THE
SECRETS
OF THE
FREEMASONS

THE
SECRETS
OF THE
FREEMASONS

PAT MORGAN

GRAMERCY BOOKS
NEW YORK

Published by Gramercy Books, an imprint of Random House
Value Publishing, a division of Random House, Inc., New York,
by arrangement with Arcturus Publishing Limited.

Gramercy is a registered trademark and the colophon
is a trademark of Random House, Inc.

Random House
New York • Toronto • London • Sydney • Auckland
www.randomhouse.com

Printed and bound in China

A catalog record for this title is available from the
Library of Congress.

ISBN-13: 978-0-517-22926-2
ISBN-10: 0-517-22926-9

10 9 8 7 6 5 4 3 2 1

Contents

INTRODUCTION

It is surprising what effect the word 'Freemason' can have when it is dropped nonchalantly into a conversation. People's reactions will vary from a raised eyebrow to a knowing look and a chuckle; from a muttered "ah yes, the Masons", to a long and embarrassed silence; from a bewildering lengthy discourse on the nature, good points and bad sides of Freemasonry to a mere puzzled shrug of the shoulders.

The truth is that the world of the Freemasons, with its strange rituals, its closely-guarded secrets, its often mysterious history and its historically low public profile, remains a puzzle to most of those who have never been accepted into its hierarchy.

Despite examination and clear explanation in many books, websites, movies, and TV and radio shows, and, in spite of the increasing openness of this global organization, its very existence is regarded with suspicion in many quarters.

The truth is that the world of the Freemasons... remains a puzzle to most of those who have never been accepted into its hierarchy

The questions from the doubters come thick and fast: who exactly are the Freemasons? Where did they come from? Just what do they get up to in those Lodges? What do those funny handshakes and weird rituals they are famed for really mean? Can women join? How do I know if someone I meet is a Freemason? Should I join if I am asked? In fact, can I simply ask to join?

In the pages of *The Secrets of the Freemasons*, we reveal the answers to these questions and many others. We explore how the organization of highly skilled medieval craftsmen led, much later, to the creation and development of an influential body of men. Furthermore, we will explore the myths and legends that shroud this fraternal group.

Discover the secrets of an often misunderstood organization, that has played a fascinating role in recent world history...

The 'evil eye' is one of the many myths associated with Freemasonry.

THE HISTORY OF FREEMASONRY

The images associated with Freemasonry, such as the square and compass that adorn countless books on the subject, may appear to some of us as symbols wrapped in mystery and conspiracy. In fact, they date back to the days when highly skilled craftsmen were building some of the astonishing cathedrals and other buildings that still dominate our cities today. They provide an important clue to the true origins of this highly subscribed and widely spread organization that exists in the modern world.

You cannot help wondering, as you gaze at some of those magnificent cathedrals of the Middle Ages, just how early builders managed to raise those huge blocks of stone to such amazing heights; how they contrived to fit them together so precisely without the benefit of modern

Nobody outside stonemason circles, not even the powerful men who employed the craftsmen to build their cathedrals, knew the secrets of the trade

technology and knowledge; and you are left contemplating just how the buildings are still standing after all these centuries.

The answer lies in geometry. The mysteries of the mathematical art were at the time known to only a very privileged few among the many who laboured long and hard to build these architectural wonders. Those few included the master craftsmen who worked in stone.

Through their knowledge of geometry, the stonemasons knew exactly what to do with the enormous rocks that came from the quarries; how they should be cut;

how to raise them; and how to keep them standing for centuries.

If you are looking for a reason why these craftsmen might be called 'free' masons, think of the huge demand for their services. They would have to be 'free' to travel from one construction site to another, unlike the men of lower skill who were obliged to serve their masters in one place.

The stonemasons, like many craftsmen of the time in Europe, were organized into guilds, and those guilds guarded the secrets of their craft jealously.

Nobody outside stonemason circles, not even the powerful men who employed them to build their cathedrals, knew the secrets of the trade. The purpose of such a guild was to ensure there were enough men schooled in the secrets and tricks of the trade – and they were all men at that time; female craftsmen would not be accepted for many centuries.

Guilds also acted as protectors of those secrets and insisted that members must uphold certain standards of workmanship.

Symbolism is used in all areas of Freemasonry. The significance of the compass, square and the letter 'G' featured here will be explained later in detail.

To become a real Mason, a young man had to progress through a lengthy seven-year apprenticeship, indentured to a Master Mason, and along the way he would be introduced to more secrets such as an initiation ceremony and signs by which he would be known to fellow Masons.

Seven years on, if the apprenticeship had gone well, the young man would become a Fellow Craft.

Then, with the passing years and the further acquisition of more experience and knowledge, he would become a Master Mason. He would now be privy to yet more secrets: the

An apprentice undergoes the initiation ceremony.

handshake, or grip, by which members would recognize each other; and the password by which other Masons would know that the man in front of them was now a respectable member of the fraternity.

Many of these processes and signs can be seen mirrored in the rituals of today's Freemasonry. They are not exactly the same, of course, for elements have inevitably changed in character over the centuries.

Nonetheless, a 21st century Mason, if he were transported back to medieval times, would undoubtedly recognize the principles and practices behind the guilds of stonemasons.

There are countless other explanations of the origins of Freemasonry, but we are discounting them to concentrate on the most accepted version.

By examining some key events, we will trace the history of the organization from the beginnings of those early guilds of stonemasons up until the present day.

1390: The Regius Manuscript

In this year, someone took on the task of describing the rules of conduct and morality by which stonemasons were expected to live. Some historians of Freemasonry believe this unknown author was merely copying from, and elaborating on, manuscripts which had been in existence even earlier, but are lost to us now.

The remarkable thing is that the framework set out in the Regius Manuscript, which today is deposited in London's British Museum, can be seen to anticipate the rules and structure of modern Freemasonry.

The document sets out a clear moral code and advocates the need for a strong brotherly bond between members. It also talks of the required standards of craftsmanship among Masons and discusses the rules of the guild. In fact, some of its phraseology would be very familiar to any Freemason today.

1495: The Word 'Freemason' Appears

The first public and official appearance of 'Freemason' came towards the end of the 15th century, when King Henry VII of England enacted some Statutes of the Realm, embodying the law of the land. Masons were highly respected members of society whose skills were much in demand, and around a century later some highborn men started to express a desire to belong to a Lodge – despite the fact that the mysteries of stone and geometry were unknown to them.

Laws passed by King Henry VII (above) included the first official appearance of the word 'Freemason' in the Statutes of the Realm in 1495.

Mixed Origins

Although the origins of Freemasonry can be traced back fairly reliably to the guilds of stonemasons, there are many other theories about its history. There are those who doubt that the origins of Freemasonry lie with these skilled, secretive craftsmen. Some observers put forward the argument that stonemasons had no need for the secret signs that are a feature of the modern organization.

Others believe that Freemasonry is descended from the Knights Templar; while some say that the history of the organization goes back no further than the 17th century.

Some Freemasons take the view that an organization of Masons existed at the time of King Athelstan, in 10th century England. It was the king, they say, who first granted a charter to Masonic Lodges in York.

It seems reasonable to accept the stonemasons theory, though. It is the one that seems to be best documented and holds up to the closest scrutiny.

The Knights Templar – the true forefathers of the Freemasons? The debate continues to this day.

17th Century: The Brotherhood Expands

Lodges in Scotland and England started to accept members who had not been instructed in the ancient craft. Many of these members, known as speculative Masons, were learned men who found the principles behind Freemasonry attractive and wanted to fully embrace the Brotherhood.

1717: The Grand Lodge of England

An historic union took place in this year. Four Lodges which met in London's Apple Tree Tavern, the Crown Ale House, the Goose and Gridiron and the Rummer and Grapes Tavern combined to form the first Grand Lodge.

A certain Anthony Sayer, who was a member of the Crown Lodge but probably knew little of the skills of masonry, was elected as the first Grand Master of the Grand Lodge of England. This act of unification was accompanied by the news, unwelcome to some, that the Grand Lodge had the sole power to grant charters to newly-formed Lodges and number them sequentially.

Grand Lodges then began to appear throughout England and, more widely, in Europe. These early groups were not without their arguments and fallings-out, for the assumed power of the Grand Lodge of England was resented in many quarters, and there were disagreements over which Lodges were the longest established – but they all served to extend the reach and the increasing popularity of Freemasonry.

These early groups were not without their arguments and fallings-out, for the assumed power of the Grand Lodge of England was resented in many quarters

1723: The Book of Constitutions

The newly-formed Grand Lodge found itself in need of some kind of constitution, and a Presbyterian minister named James Anderson was charged with the task of setting out the rules of Freemasonry. This he did with the *Book of Constitutions*, and the guidelines set out in it have been followed, with varying degrees of conformity, ever since.

One of the most interesting guidelines set out in the publication concerned religion. Anderson's words made it clear that, although Freemasons were obliged to believe in God, or at least a 'Supreme Being', if they wanted to join, they were free to subscribe to whatever religion they wanted.

God was referred to during Masonic rituals as the Grand Architect of the Universe. All faiths were thus welcome to join the Freemason movement.

1753: The Antients' Breakaway

Disputes arose over whether the Grand Lodge of England was serving Freemasonry properly, and a breakaway Lodge was formed. Antients, whose members came by and large from the working classes, formed their own Grand Lodge in 1753.

They believed the rituals enacted in a Lodge should reflect those practiced in the golden age of Masonry, while the so-called Moderns – for the most part the 'gentleman' type of Freemason – wanted a more philosophical approach stressing the principles of brotherly love, charity and truth. There were also disagreements over the Masonic modes of recognition – in other words, the secret signs by which Freemasons knew each other.

1813: The United Grand Lodge of England

The dispute was settled by compromise, and the Antients and Moderns came together to form the United Grand Lodge of England. The modes of recognition were restored to what they had been before 1753 and there was finally agreement over the identity of the degrees of Freemasonry (see following page).

By this time, Lodges had been springing up all over the British Isles, in Europe and in British colonies, including America. Members of the nobility in many countries, and even royalty, had embraced the fraternity with enthusiasm and this in turn made Freemasonry ever more attractive – and a target for controversy.

An engraving from circa 1850 which lists the Freemasonry Lodges in London and the provincial areas.

The Three Degrees

When the United Grand Lodge of England (UGLE) was formed in 1813, the so-called Antient and Modern factions came to an agreement over what should be the three degrees of Freemasonry. Members progressing through their life in the fraternity find themselves in one of three degrees: Entered Apprentice, Fellow Craft or Master Mason.

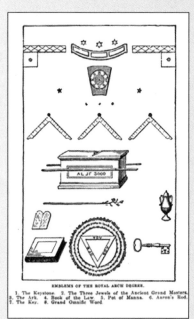

EMBLEMS OF THE ROYAL ARCH DEGREE.
1. The Keystone. 2. The Three Jewels of the Ancient Grand Masters. 3. The Ark. 4. Book of the Law. 5. Pot of Manna. 6. Aaron's Rod. 7. The Key. 8. Grand Omnific Word.

The Royal Arch degree, which caused much debate when introduced.

What all this in practice means varies from country to country and even from Lodge to Lodge – and we will examine the whole issue of degrees in a later chapter – but the compromise that enabled the formation of the UGLE made it clear that these three degrees formed the basis of Freemasonry.

The Antients had been working on the principle that there was a higher degree – the Antient Royal Arch – and they were allowed to regard this as the completion of the third degree. The Moderns, however, looked on the Antient Royal Arch as very much an optional higher degree.

The Female Sex

Freemasonry has always had more than its fair share of opponents, and they have sometimes included women. Although early Freemasons were exclusively male, Elizabeth Aldworth was admitted as a member of an Irish Lodge in the early 18th century, after spying on a ceremony. Disgruntled members were obliged to initiate her, and she was even granted a Masonic burial when she died.

Over the centuries, women's organizations imitating Masonic Lodges have been set up and have been successful, but it was in France that women made the greatest progress establishing themselves in early Freemasonry.

In 1882, Maria Deraismes was initiated into the Loge Libre Penseurs (Free Thinkers) and the Lodge went on to admit 16 female members. Nowadays, most Grand Lodges accept that women can play some kind of part in Freemasonry, and there are also many thriving associated bodies that admit only women.

Elizabeth Aldworth – the first woman to enter the Freemasons.

The William Morgan Scandal

The history of Freemasonry has never been without its controversies for very long, and one of the biggest – surrounding the unknown fate of a member – started in 1826.

That year, an American Mason by the name of William Morgan disappeared. Suspicions that Freemasons might have been involved were strengthened by the fact that Morgan, seemingly disillusioned with the Brotherhood, was apparently at work on a book that would lay bare the organization's secrets.

Those suspicions were well founded: some Masons in the state of New York, outraged by Morgan's anti-Masonic conduct, said they had abducted the unfortunate man, escorted him to the Canadian border, given him $500 and told him never to darken America's door again.

No one was ever tried for murder, but six men were charged over the disappearance. The sentences handed down were considered light in some quarters, and there was uproar as it became apparent that the prosecutors and some jurors were Freemasons.

Rumours spread like wildfire across the States. It was alleged that Morgan's life had been ended during an appalling Masonic ritual. There were claims that Freemasons controlled the entire judiciary and ruling classes and looked after their own.

The incident sparked off widespread anti-Masonic protests, fuelled by the publication of Morgan's book. These actions included attacks on Lodges, the formation of anti-Masonic political parties and the insistence that any participation in Freemasonry was an anti-American activity.

The picture shows a re-enactment of what some believe happened to Morgan. Because of the scandal, Freemason membership plummeted with some members taking their affiliations to other organizations, and it took time for the fraternity to regain its popularity, especially in the US.

19th and 20th Centuries: Growth

While views have differed through the centuries about exactly what Freemasonry should be about, who should be admitted and which rituals should be followed, with the result that, today, practices vary widely across the world, the movement still remains strong.

The growth of Freemasonry has been steady over the centuries, with some spectacular bursts of activity at certain times, and today there are an estimated five million Masons in the world.

The spread of Freemasonry has not been without its dark moments. Hitler suggested that the fraternity was no more than a front for the Jews who he claimed were seeking to destroy the existing world order. Everywhere the Nazi blitzkrieg machine moved in World War II, Lodges were sacked and Freemasons were rounded up and sent off, often to their deaths, to the concentration camps.

Hitler suggested that the Freemasons were no more than a front for the Jews who he claimed were seeking to destroy the existing world order

The end of the war saw a clearly-defined upswing in the fortunes of Freemasonry. Membership in the United States alone reached more than four million just 14 years after the war in 1959. But the 1960s and 1970s saw a decline in interest because of the growing 'generation gap' between those who had known the horrors of war and their offspring, and rival attractions such as TV and pop music. It took the digital revolution that united the world through the internet to bring about a renaissance.

Now, thanks to email and websites, Freemasons throughout the world communicate with each other – and with the outside world – freely and easily, making the challenge of recruiting new members a much simpler task.

As a result, the numbers lost from the fraternity from the 1960s onwards are being slowly and steadily restored.

But what of the future? Will Freemasonry hold on to its important position in the world of tomorrow?

The enduring nature of the Freemasons is reflected in its architecture – pictured above is the Masonic Temple of the Scottish Rite in Washington DC.

SECRETS AND BLOOD TIES

Reading a brief history of the Masons does not bring us any closer to permeating their secretive world of rituals, secret signs and strange handshakes. To understand what it means to be a Freemason today requires an analysis of their belief system and a look at the structure of their famous Lodges.

As with anything that is kept behind closed doors, the practices and beliefs of the Freemasons are matters of curiosity for anyone not in the know. This secrecy is also the main reason for many of the rumours and untruths that have been whispered about the Masons, as people are often afraid of what they do not know or cannot understand. To add to the confusion, there are also the so-called 'appendant and concordant bodies', which can have similar practices to the Freemasons but different history and reasoning.

As an organization that makes much of meaning and symbolism, for the Freemasons there is reason behind every decision, from where people sit in the Lodges to what badges they wear. And, as with any body that has a worldwide membership, some practices vary between locations and Lodges.

Although the complex structure of the Freemasons and the 'appendant and concordant bodies' can be difficult to follow at first, all should become clear in the following pages.

As with anything that is kept behind closed doors, the practices and beliefs of the Freemasons are matters of curiosity for anyone not in the know

Men of unimpeachable character, such as George Washington, have long formed the backbone of the Freemasons and given the organization respectibility in the face of public suspicion and hostility.

Being a Freemason

The concept behind Freemasonry is hard to explain, but one thing it is not is a religion. It has, however, elements in common with most religions, in particular there is a code of behaviour or ethics.

Freemasonry is more than just a secret fraternity; it is a system of morals, a philosophy, if you will. It is a kind of way to lead your life. Freemasons are men who have sworn to abide by laws and customs that are directly descended from the rules of the ancient guild of stonemasons.

As they progress through the degrees of Freemasonry, Masons learn social and moral values that are based on the symbolism of the tools of the ancient stonemasons and their language

As they progress through the degrees of Freemasonry, Masons learn social and moral values that are based on the symbolism of the tools of the ancient stonemasons, and their language. They learn, also, that the construction of a building can be likened to the building of character.

Freemasons swear to abide by the precepts of the organization: they must show brotherly love to their fellow humans; they must offer assistance to their Brothers in times of need; they must accept the principles of trust, secrecy and equality. They must be tolerant of their fellow man's beliefs. They learn to recognize other Masons by the means of secret handshakes (or grips), passwords and signs.

Freemasonry is not dogmatic: Masons are not told what to believe. Members must possess a belief in the existence of a Supreme Being. It follows that a Christian can be a Freemason, as can a Muslim or a Jew.

Freemasons through the ages have believed in showing brotherly love to fellow humans.

Freemasons have been showing themselves in public for many decades – here Major R Lawrence Thornton, Worshipful Provincial Grand Master of the Freemasons, lays the foundation stone of the Sussex Eye Hospital during a ceremony in Brighton, England, in 1933.

Masons refer to the Supreme Being as the Grand Architect of the Universe. Note that that appellation could encompass almost any religious belief, and note also that this absence of a 'Masonic God' means that neither is there a 'Masonic Devil'.

Just as Freemasonry does not tell its members which version of God to believe in, neither does it tell them what to believe about anything else. It does, however, encourage learning, thereby urging Masons to make up their own minds about the world.

As you would expect of an organization whose members are expected to uphold high moral standards and regard their fellow men as equals, Freemasonry is active in charitable works.

Many a charity project has benefited from the work of members of a Lodge, and those occasions when that work makes the pages of the local newspaper may be among the few times when you recognize a face and think, "Oh, so he's a Mason."

There may be other occasions when Freemasons show a public face. Sometimes, when a Mason dies, the grieving family will request that his Lodge perform a memorial service.

Sometimes Freemasons are asked to perform an opening ceremony to mark the laying of the cornerstone of an important building – this is the most obvious demonstration of the medieval origins of Freemasonry that you are ever likely to see.

Those two examples show the public face of Freemasonry, but there is, of course, the more hidden aspect of the organization. So what exactly are Masonic Lodges, and what goes on inside them?

Freemasonry is active in charitable works. Many a charity project has benefited from the work of members of a Lodge

The Lodge

Practices in a Lodge vary from country to country, from state to state, even from one Lodge to another. Each country, or state, has a kind of governing body, or Grand Lodge, and individual Lodges look up to the Grand Lodge for guidance.

Each Lodge has a number, and these numbers are issued by the Grand Lodge in strict sequence, so if a Lodge has a low number, it indicates that it has been in existence for a very long time.

The word 'Lodge' can refer both to the organization of men, on a local, regional or national level and to the buildings in which they meet.

The word 'lodge' comes from the French 'loge', which is related to 'logement': habitation or accommodation

In days gone by, stonemasons would meet in a building close to the site of their work, where they could mingle, discuss their tasks, and learn from their fellows. The word 'lodge' comes from the French 'loge', which is related to 'logement'; meaning habitation.

What will you find inside a Lodge? If Freemasons could return in time to the Temple of Solomon, they might find some of the features very familiar, for many of the contents and layout of a Lodge building are based on the descriptions of that building.

The Lodge room is constructed so that the entrance door is toward the west. Thus, as one enters, one is facing east. This is of symbolic significance since temples in the time of Solomon were built in alignment with the passage of the sun.

Built in 1932 in Virginia, the George Washington Masonic National Monument acts as a Lodge and a fitting tribute to the former president and his work in the Freemasons.

This is the Freemason's Temple built in 1912 at the Great Eastern Hotel in London, England.

As you would expect of people who are said to be 'on the square', the Lodge has four sides, and its seating is arranged around the outside of the room. The Lodge contains a Volume of Sacred Law, open upon an altar. This does not have to be the *Bible*; it could be the *Qur'an* or any other sacred text, as long as it signifies the Lodge members' belief in a Supreme Being.

The Volume of Sacred Law is illuminated by three candles (the importance of the number three to Masons is covered in the next chapter), placed in a triangular formation around the altar. The room will feature two globes set on the top of two pillars. These are symbolic of the pillars of the Temple of Solomon. The pillars will be placed next to the entrance door, or erhaps on either side of the Senior Warden's chair.

How else would you recognize that you are in a Masonic Lodge? The letter 'G' hangs over the Master's chair or over the altar. As we will see in a later chapter, the 'G' is a representation of God and of

geometry, the science whose secrets the original masons guarded so closely.

The Senior Warden sits on a chair in the west of the Lodge while the Worshipful Master sits in the east. The Senior Warden's chair is on a platform featuring two steps, while the Junior Warden's platform has one step. Together, these three steps symbolize the three stages of life: youth, manhood and age.

There, with a little imagination you can now envisage a Lodge building – a building whose interior most people will never see.

The Lodge contains a Volume of Sacred Law, open upon an altar... it signifies the Lodge members' belief in a Supreme Being

---

The Officers

Although the officer structure may vary slightly between Lodges, the following will give a idea of how Masonic Lodges are structured. It will also outline the duties and responsibilities of the different officers and the significance behind their badges of office.

Pride of place goes to the Worshipful Master, who sits on his chair where the sun rises, in the east of the Lodge.

The Worshipful Master is a worldly and experienced Mason. It is his job to preside over meetings and to confer degrees. Each hierarchy has a particular badge of office (or jewel). The Worshipful Master's is a right angle of a square, worn around his neck. This harks back to the days of the original stonemasons, who used a right angle to check the geometric properties of the stone they were working with. In the case of the Lodge's Worshipful Master, it is a symbol of virtue.

The Senior Warden of the Lodge is the second in command. His chair is placed towards the setting sun, in the west. His jewel of office is a level, which ancient stonemasons used to ensure their surfaces were level, and its symbolic meaning is that all

Masons are equal. His role in Lodge meetings is to assist the Worshipful Master in the execution of his duties, and deputize for him if need be.

In third position in the Lodge's pecking order is the Junior Warden, whose jewel of office is a plumb. A plumb was used to ensure that the building was truly upright, so it symbolizes an upright moral attitude. The Junior Warden sits in the south where the sun is at noon – and his tasks include the provision of refreshment for members, an appropriate duty for one who symbolizes midday.

The Worshipful Master is a worldly and experienced Mason

Freemason Jean Charles Foellner is the Worshipful Master of the Grand Lodge Nationale Française in Paris, France.

The nearest British equivalent of a Junior Deacon is a Grand Tyler. He stands here in full uniform at the United Grand Lodge of Freemasons in England.

The Senior Deacon's jewel is a square and compass, the symbol most often associated in the public's mind with Freemasonry. The sun sits in the middle of the square and compass, and the Senior Deacon sits in the east, to the Worshipful Master's right. Another accoutrement of this office is a long rod, on top of which the square and compass is affixed.

The Senior Deacon's job is to welcome candidates and visitors, to guide candidates around the Lodge, to open and close the Volume of Sacred Law at the beginning and end of meetings, and to light and douse the candles.

The Junior Deacon also has a square and compass as his badge of office, and it is also carried on a rod. However, there is no sun inside the symbol; instead, the Junior Deacon has a moon. He sits to the Senior Warden's right and one of his tasks is to act as guardian of the Lodge's door.

This entails a lot of knocking on the door, to ascertain who is outside and whether they are fit to enter the confines of the Lodge. We are now coming towards the end of the Lodge officers who are in a 'progressive line', meaning that they move up one place in the hierarchy once a year. Thus the next officer on our list, the Senior Steward has a few years to serve before he becomes Worshipful Master.

The Senior Steward shares a jewel of office with the Junior Steward. It is a horn of plenty, or cornucopia, atop a rod, and it signifies that they help in the preparation of Lodge meals. Other tasks of the stewards include preparing the Lodge for meetings.

The Lodge's monetary affairs and administrative tasks are entrusted to the treasurer and the secretary. These officers are not in the progressive line.

The treasurer, whose jewel (crossed keys) shows he is in charge of petty cash, sits to the right of the Worshipful Master. The secretary sits to the Master's left and carries out vital administrative tasks necessary to keep an organization like a Masonic Lodge running. His jewel of office is a pair of crossed quill pens.

Meetings

Degree ceremonies attract most curiosity from non-Masons because of their ritual but there are many other Masonic meetings that go on, from week to week throughout the year, that are much less esoteric. We are going to look at the ritual at some ceremonies later in this book; this section concerns itself with day-to-day events.

Lodge meetings may involve listening to a guest speaker or a fellow Mason instructing members on what it means to be a Freemason. Few Lodge meetings are held without some kind of food and beverage offering, called the 'festive board'. All foodstuffs and drink are taken in moderation, for a good Freemason does nothing to excess.

As ever, how things are done varies from place to place, and things can get even more different in the organizations the Masons call concordant and appendant bodies, and in other organizations with which Freemasonry has been linked.

Lodge meetings may involve listening to a guest speaker or a fellow Mason instructing members on what being a Freemason is all about

A photograph of the 1992 annual meeting of the Freemasons held in London, England.

Politically Incorrect

Every internet fan must surely have come across the sites that proclaim
the world is governed secretly by an elite of men. At the heart of this top
secret conspiracy are the Freemasons, the websites whisper. Freemasons
rule the world and have a say in everything you are allowed, or not
allowed, to do, they say. It will not be long before the truth is revealed
and we see the Masons for what they are really like.

If the website authors were to do some real investigation, they would find
out that Masons are not permitted to talk politics in the confines of their

Lodges. It is rather naïve to believe that a New World Order could be organized and planned and its imposition be created without the instigators strenuously engaging in politics.

It is true that a fair few men in positions of political power throughout the world are Freemasons. It has always been that way, since the early days of modern Freemasonry. It is also true that a lot of painters, used car dealers, insurance salesmen, realtors, shopping mall managers and piano-removal men are Freemasons. Are they in on the conspiracy too?

Do Freemasons rule the world, as conspiracy theorists claim?

Other Bodies

As well as the three degrees of Entered Apprentice, Fellow Craft and Master Mason, there are other bodies which can confer other degrees of progression through the fraternity.

As with everything to do with Freemasonry, there are complicating factors, and here they come in the form of the concordant and appendant bodies.

Concordant means 'in agreement' while appendant means 'hanging on'. These bodies are associated with Freemasonry although their practices may differ quite distinctly. An example of an appendant body is the Ancient Accepted Scottish Rite, which can confer further degrees on a Master Mason, numbering up to 32 and, very occasionally, 33 as a mark of extraordinary service.

The Scottish Rite was developed mainly on the continent of Europe, and especially in France.

It was in the middle of the 18th century that a Scot, Andrew Ramsay, proclaimed that Freemasonry was an ancient import to Scotland from the crusades in the Middle East.

His ideas were accepted with enthusiasm and French Masons set to work to flesh them out, in the process coming up with an increasing number of degrees. The new degrees became known as Scottish, although their origins are not in that part of Great Britain.

The Scottish Rite crossed the Atlantic Ocean and found a fertile breeding ground in the New World. Today in the United States, it is divided into two jurisdictions: the Southern Masonic Jurisdiction and the Northern Masonic Jurisdiction. In spite of its popularity many Masons choose not to become involved with the Scottish Rite.

The Scottish Rite crossed the Atlantic Ocean and found a fertile breeding ground in the New World

The Scottish Rite Masonic Temple in Miami, Florida.

Another appendant body is the York Rite. As we have seen, in the early decades of modern Freemasonry there were those who were not above adding a few degrees to the basic three.

In England, a group of men came together to add some higher degrees, which have become known across the Atlantic as the York Rite.

This title covers three distinct rites: the Holy Royal Arch, Cryptic Masonry and Chivalric. The Knights Templar can be found in the Chivalric order.

It would be ridiculous to assume that the 33rd degree of the Scottish Rite shows the bearer is 11 times better than a Master Mason

Between them, these groups confer ten degrees, with which a Master Mason can enlarge his learning if he should so desire.

It is very important to note here that the degrees offered by the Scottish Rite and the York Rite are additional to the three basic degrees every Masonic candidate will eventually learn about.

They are not considered any better than those degrees; it would be ridiculous to assume, for example, that the 33rd degree of the Scottish Rite shows the bearer is 11 times better than a Master Mason. They are simply additions.

Other concordant and appendant bodies include the Ancient Arabic Nobles of the Mystic Shrine, better known to the world at large as the Shriners.

The Shrine is probably the most popular appendant body of Freemasonry. It grew out of the regular convivial meetings, toward the end of the 19th century, of New York

The Knights Templar hold a Palm Sunday procession in Jerusalem, Israel.

City Masons, who opted for less formal meetings, making their Lodge a more sociable body. Picking up some knowledge of the Middle East and Arabic, they formed a lively group, hailed each other with the greeting 'Es Selamu Aleikum', and adopted a red fez as their headgear.

Growth of the Shriners among established Freemasons was fairly rapid right across the States, and they became known not only for their fezzes and parades but also for the good works they performed. Beginning by raising money for less fortunate children, they proceeded to open and operate hospitals, which now number more than 20 across the US and offer free medical care.

There are many other appendant and concordant bodies associated with Freemasonry. They include so-called androgynous groups, where a male Mason can attend with his female relations: the likes of the Daughters of the Nile, the White Shrine of Jerusalem and the Order of the Eastern Star.

There are other groups, apart from the Shriners, whose emphasis focuses on sociability. They include the Tall Cedars of Lebanon, the veterans' organization the National Sojourners, and the Grotto, more formally known as the Mystic Order of the Veiled Prophets of the Enchanted Realm.

Growth of the Shriners among established Freemasons was fairly rapid right across the States

A Shriner sporting a red fez.

Then there are the youth groups, which for the most part are for the children of Freemasons, and from whose ranks they sometimes graduate to become fully-fledged Masons. For example, girls are catered for by the International Order of the Rainbow and Job's Daughters, while young men can join DeMolay International.

There are many organizations, societies and associations which are mistakenly linked to the Freemasons such as the Odd Fellows and the highly respected Moose International

Every single one of these groups is open to Freemasons, or the relations of Freemasons. And there are many more of similar character.

Many associations, societies, clubs and fraternal organizations exist without having any link to Freemasonry although it may be believed that they are some kind of cover for the Masons.

Examples are the UK's Knights of St Columba (motto: Serve God by Serving Others), the Odd Fellows (the 'Three Link' fraternity, standing for friendship, love and truth) and Moose International (1.5 million men and women in four nations dedicated to bettering the lives of children and the elderly in need). None of this is linked to Freemasonry.

They may look like Masons but the Odd Fellows fraternity is not actually related to the Freemason organization.

The Truth about the Knights Templar

Are the Knights Templar not the ones who have guarded the Ark of the Covenant and other treasures since Biblical times? They are the jealous guardians of other secrets of global importance, too. We know, because we have seen the movie *National Treasure*, and we have read *The Da Vinci Code*.

However, as always, the truth is a little less glamorous than the conspiracy theorists would have you believe. Today's Knights Templar, in the United States at least, confer to the three chivalric degrees of the York Rite, known as 'orders'. They are the Illustrious Order of the Red Cross, the Order of Malta and the Order of the Temple. It is important to note that candidates for this Masonic order must be of Christian faith.

How did this confusion arise? It all goes back to Andrew Ramsay's 18th century story circulating in France about Freemasonry originating from the original Knights Templar, the crusading knights who defended Jerusalem from the Saracens. This order of pious Christian knights made its home close to the Temple of Solomon, and chevaliers returning from the Holy Land brought news of them. This, said Ramsay, contained the real origins of Freemasonry. There is not even a grain of truth in the story as far as most dispassionate observers are concerned, but it makes a good tale.

The original Knights' spiritual successors say that they have no idea of the whereabouts of the Ark of the Covenant, the Holy Grail or any other artifacts from ancient Biblical times.

The Masonic Knights Templar have nothing to do with the Knights Templar of old who were said to guard the Holy Grail.

SECRET SIGNS

Freemasons have long had a reputation for participating in odd ceremonies involving aprons, secret handshakes, rolled-up trouser legs and esoteric symbols. But what do all those strange symbols mean? And why on earth do they wear those aprons? Is what we hear about their mysterious rituals really true or just the stuff of gossip?

This chapter sets out to answer these seemingly perplexing questions. There are plenty of surprises in store because the reasons behind the seemingly strange and bizarre rituals are firmly based in logic and reason. There is no doubt that we will also be disappointing a minority; the kind of people who believe the symbols used by Masons are insidious signs of a twisted organization, or one that does not have the best interests of its fellow citizens at heart.

They were an elite who felt strongly that it was in the best interests of the Craft to keep the secrets of their success close to their chests

Whatever your take on the Masons though, there is still plenty in the signs, symbolism and rituals of Freemasonry that is fascinating.

We have already seen that much of the secret stuff associated with this hushed fraternal organization can be traced back to its origins among the medieval stonemasons who practiced a highly-skilled craft and took care not to let the uninitiated know too much about what they were up to.

After all, they were, in a way, an elite who felt strongly that it was in the best interests of the Craft to keep the secrets of their success close to their chests. It wouldn't do to let just anyone in on centuries of hard earned knowledge, technique and skill. So let us examine in detail the all-important symbols that lie at the heart of Freemasonry, and uncover their hidden meaning.

A Freemason in all his regalia – but the dress code is the least important aspect of becoming a member of the fraternity.

Symbols

Many symbols associated with Freemasonry have their origins in the tools of the trade of the medieval stonemasons, and they are very often mathematical in nature. Interpretations of them sometimes vary. Here is what is actually known.

The best-known of these symbols are the square and compass, which are laid out so as to form a four-sided figure, or quadrilateral. When you look at these two tools, it is easy to imagine the original 'operative' Masons using them in the execution of their work.

What is the significance of the humble compass to the modern Freemason? It represents the fraternal nature of Freemasonry. But how? As ever with this organization, it depends on who you ask

The square was used to ensure angles in stone were 'on the square' as they were worked and placed in position.

The two arms linked by the joint of the compass, which is used for drawing circles and arcs and measuring distances between two points, have an obvious role in stonemasonry.

What is their meaning to modern Freemasons? Put simply, they represent the fraternal nature of Freemasonry. But how? As ever with this organization, it depends on who you ask.

It is explained to Masons as they start their progress through the degrees that the square stands for all that is fair, honest and virtuous, ensuring that everything fits together as it is meant to according to the grand plan. Some Freemasons say the square represents matter, the concrete stuff of which the world is actually composed.

The compass, according to the same people, represents the world of the abstract. The principles of Freemasonry – fraternal love, friendship and morality – are contained between the two points of the tool. The point of the compass that remains steady and constant at the center as a circle is drawn can be said to stand for a single Mason, while the point that describes the circle represents all of Freemasonry and the limits of the world. The individual Mason must remain within these limits at all times.

Together the compass and the square form the basis of all Freemasonry symbolism.

In the space between the square and compass, you will often find another symbol: a star, an eye or the letter 'G'.

The letter 'G' is said to stand for God, Freemasons being required to believe in a Supreme Being. Others point out that 'G' can also stand for 'Geometry'. Other symbols sometimes found in the space between the square and the compass are an all-seeing eye, a moon and stars, or a sun. These are interpreted as symbols of light, truth and knowledge – of God, if you like.

It is a commonly held belief that God can see into the hearts of men, and Christians have used the eye as a religious symbol for many centuries

The use of the letter 'G' stands for 'God'.

The all-seeing eye is another representation of God.

The all-seeing eye refers to the belief that God can see into the hearts of men, and Christians have used the eye as a religious symbol for many centuries. The all-seeing eye is often depicted within a triangle, for the number three is significant within the Freemasons community.

The triangle represents the three elements of the Holy Trinity – Father, Son and Holy Spirit – and much of Masonic life and its rituals make reference to this number: there are three degrees in a Lodge, three underlying principles of Freemasonry, and so on.

The triangle represents the Holy Trinity.

The aprons worn by Freemasons are replete with symbolism. First of all, they are reminders of the stonemason's ancient craft, for the original masons wore aprons to store tools and protect their clothing.

Given to a Freemason at the start of his progress through the degrees, the apron is traditionally made from lambskin because the innocent young lamb is regarded as a symbol of untainted purity. A Mason, whether he is wearing the apron or not, must constantly conduct his life with purity in mind; he must always strive for unblemished perfection in thought, action and deed.

Symbols embroidered onto the aprons include the eye of God or the compass and square, the symbolism of which we have examined on previous pages.

The apron remains with the Mason for all time, such is its importance – even accompanying him to the grave.

Other tools of the stonemason's trade are often used as symbols, and these include the trowel, used to lay mortar between stones. For Freemasons, the trowel is symbolic of the spreading of the message of fraternal love, and of the cementing together of like-minded people in a Lodge.

The trowel represents fraternal love.

The chisel symbolizes perfection.

The famous aprons worn by Freemasons are reminders of the stonemason's ancient craft.

The level stands for equality.

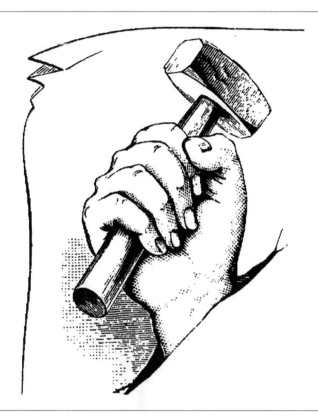

Further symbols deriving from ancient stonemasonry abound in today's Lodges: the hammer, which symbolizes chipping away at members' rough edges; the 24-inch gauge, reminding Masons of the hours in a day; the chisel, symbolic of perfection in work; the plumb, which measures the perpendicular and symbolizes the upstanding nature of Masonic philosophy; and last, but not least, the level, which ensures surfaces are absolutely horizontal, stands for equality among fellow Brothers.

As we have seen in a previous chapter, the Biblical story of the Temple of King Solomon in Jerusalem – built by King Solomon with the help of Master Masons and utterly destroyed by the marauding and murderous Babylonian King Nebuchadnezzar – has particular resonance for Freemasons, and its symbolism is very important. The construction of the temple is embodied in an individual Mason making his way through the degrees, but its destruction will follow if he abandons his faith, his belief and his direction.

The King Solomon link continues – the symbolism of the pillars found in all sorts of Masonic illustrations hark back to the pillars that stood at the entrance to the Temple of King Solomon and represent solidity and endurance, and real pillars, erected in Lodge buildings, play a major role in the ceremony of the Fellow Craft degree.

The link with King Solomon is very strong within Masonic culture.

Time waits for no man.

Finally, the shortness of life is often symbolized by an hourglass, with its sands slipping away. An hourglass is often held by the Grim Reaper, who also wields a scythe to do his work.

Much has been written on the symbols of Freemasonry, but we will move on to the secret signs that make Freemasonry such a mystery to outsiders.

Meeting and Greeting

The hand shakes are probably the best known of the Freemasons' secret signs. They were devised for good reason, at a time when being a Mason was punishable by death. Before we look at the various types shown below, you should know that an 'Entered Apprentice' has passed the initiation; 'Fellow Craft' is a Brother who has taken on the Lodge's obligations; and a 'Master Mason' is what all Brothers aspire to become.

'The Grip of the Entered Apprentice' – the Mason presses his thumb against the top of the first knuckle-joint of the fellow Mason, with the fellow Mason pressing his thumb against the first Mason's knuckle.

'The Real Grip of a Fellow Craft' – the Mason takes the fellow Mason by the right hand, and then presses the top of his thumb hard on the second knuckle. At the same time, the fellow Mason presses his thumb against the same knuckle of the first Mason's hand.

'The Real Grip of a Master Mason' – the Mason firmly grasps the right hand of a fellow Mason, the thumbs of both hands interlaced. The first Mason presses the tops of his fingers against the wrist of the fellow Mason where it meets with the hand. At the same time, the fellow Mason presses his own fingers against the corresponding part of the first Mason's hand with each finger splayed. This grip is also known as the 'Lion's Paw'.

If a Mason sees a fellow Brother making this sign, he must intervene at once and help.

Sign Language

There are other signs that a Mason will learn as he ascends the ranks: the sign of horror (dropping as if afflicted by a dreadful sight); the sign of sympathy (a gentle smiting of the forehead with the palm of the right hand); and the penal sign (drawing the hand across the body).

There are still others: the sign of grief (passing the hand across the forehead); and the sign of joy and exultation, sometimes called the 'grand' or 'royal' sign (first given by Solomon when his temple was at last finished and he was struck by its wonders). As with all things Masonic, there is variation in signs between Lodges, and the same can be said of the rituals enacted at Lodge meetings.

The use of passwords in Freemasonry is yet another cornerstone of the Brotherhood. Accompanying the grip that must be learnt by the apprentice, is learning about the password, which consists of the spelled-out letters BOAZ. The initiate is asked for this password as the ritual progresses.

The word is symbolic of strength and alludes to the name of the left-hand pillar at the entrance to the Temple of King Solomon, as well as to the

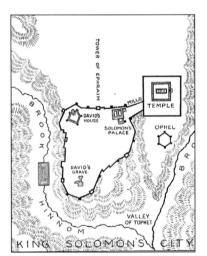

A map of King Solomon's City – the Temple itself plays an important part in the ceremonies and initiations of the Freemasons.

great-grandfather of the Biblical King David.

There are other passwords familiar to Freemasons everywhere, although rituals and signs are just as variable in Lodges throughout the world as every other aspect of Freemasonry.

Spelling out the word JACHIN, another password and the name of the right-hand pillar in King Solomon's temple, forms part of the ritual that accompanies the passing to the second degree of Freemasonry, that of Fellow Craft. Jachin was the priest who officiated at the ceremony of dedication of Solomon's temple.

There is another password that is fairly current in the public domain and is also spelled out during the Fellow Craft ritual: SHIBBOLETH. It denotes 'plenty' and, like the other passwords, dates back to the time of King Solomon.

Knowledge of this password during the building of the temple would have enabled the speaker to ascend a staircase leading to the middle chamber.

Over the centuries and with the growth of Freemasonry – and that of similar offshoots – variations on handshakes and other symbolic gestures have been introduced and become established

Among these is a way of standing. The Worshipful Master, during a ceremony of initiation, will instruct the initiate to stand perfectly erect, with his feet formed into a square – the Freemason's favorite shape.

The upstanding body is considered a symbol of the mind while the position of the feet denotes the moral rectitude required of a Mason.

Nowadays, it is a sign that one is privy to some of the secrets of Freemasonry. In the the Masonic world, there are countless variations on the grips, handshakes and passwords that we have mentioned here.

Over the centuries and with the growth of the organization – and that ofsimilar organizations and offshoots – variations have been introduced and become established. Many of them will remain secret.

As with the gestures by which Freemasons make their presence known to their Brothers, there are some that are known to non-Masons.

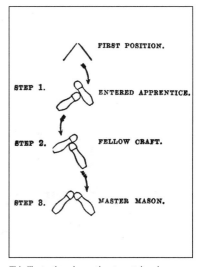

This illustration shows the steps taken by Freemasons during ceremonies to physically show the three degrees of the Brotherhood.

Rituals

They are elaborate; they are mysterious to the uninitiated; they relate back to ancient happenings; and they are secret. The ceremonies of Freemasonry, called rituals and acted out to mark the passage of Masons from one degree to the next as well as being used in more mundane matters, make much of the signs, grips and passwords already described. They also make use of Biblical imagery, the tools of the stonemason's trade, arcane and archaic language, and strange behaviour. The best known example of this is the rolling up of the trouser leg. What is the history behind the rituals?

At his initiation, the candidate will in all probability find himself dressed in a way he would probably never have considered before: with one shoe off, a trouser leg and a shirtsleeve rolled up, his left breast exposed, a blindfold (or hoodwink) over his head and a rope (or cable-tow) round his neck.

In the olden days, a stonemason would use a rope called a cable-tow to climb to great heights on a building and to raise his tools up to that height too.

The candidate's left breast is exposed because the point of a 'poniard', or small dagger, is applied to that area of the body. A leg is exposed to accentuate the sense of danger implicit in this action. He is blindfolded, or hoodwinked, because he is at that point symbolically in the darkness, seeking admission to enlightenment, and he must not yet be allowed to see the interior of the Lodge building.

The symbolism of the rolled-up trouser leg is important, too. It is meant to represent a suit of rags, and implies that, whatever his wealth, the candidate seeking admission to the Lodge will be equal to all other Masons. In fact, many Lodges in Freemasonry today provide the candidate with specially-prepared clothing so he does not have to go through the hassle of baring a leg and breast while in his normal clothes. The suitably-dressed candidate knocks at the door of the

Lodge and is, after a ritual exchange of words, allowed in. He is then led in a procession through the Lodge room and questioned by its various officers as to his motives and his suitability as an Entered Apprentice.

All the time he is moving around, or circumambulating, our initiate is doing so in a definite, prescribed manner: in straight lines, forming a square as his progress is completed. Finally, he is conducted to the altar, where he kneels and takes the obligation, or oath, promising not to reveal Masonic secrets to outsiders. The penalties outlined in the obligation can be quite severe (see page 67).

Having sworn to abide by the code of the Freemasons, the candidate then has his blindfold and rope removed. The candidate is then allowed to see the interior of the Lodge building for the very first time. The signs and grips of the Entered Apprentice are revealed to him and he is presented with his white lambskin apron, to be cherished and treasured for evermore. Furthermore the importance to Freemasons of charity and of brotherly love is impressed upon him. Another Entered Apprentice has been created.

What a candidate wears during his initiation process is steeped in symbolism – the rolled-up trouser leg, bared breast, blindfold and rope.

As with all Freemason rituals, the candidate must follow a strict order of movement during the initiation process.

Quiet Please

There is a rather dramatic point during the ritual of initiation that has been seized on by anti-Masons and conspiracy theorists.

The candidate, having already had a dagger applied to his breast and had a rope looped noose-like round his neck, is asked to swear that, as a man of honor, he would rather have his throat cut than reveal the secrets of the fraternity.

Similar oaths accompany Fellow Craft and Master Mason rituals. The fate of the treacherous Fellow Craft is to have his heart torn from his breast and fed to ravenous birds, while the Master Mason is threatened with being cut in two and then having his bowels burned.

Freemasons insist that such penalties were never actually enforced in the past. And to ensure that no one continued to get the wrong idea, the macabre punishment was removed from the oaths back in 1986.

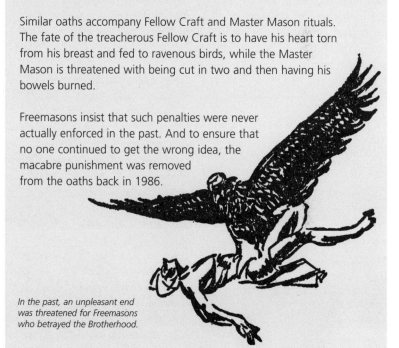

In the past, an unpleasant end was threatened for Freemasons who betrayed the Brotherhood.

Rituals for higher degrees have many similarities to that for Entered Apprentices. New grips, signs and passwords are revealed during the ceremony for the next degree – the Fellow Craft. The ceremony of the highest degree in Freemasonry, the Master Mason, is more dramatic.

Part of this ceremony takes the form of a presentation of the death of Hiram Abiff, who held the esteemed position of Master Architect of King Solomon's Temple.

Hiram was one day set upon by three fellows of the Craft who longed to know the secrets of a Master Mason, and used the tools of their trade to do the man to death

The unfortunate Hiram was one day set upon by three fellows of the Craft who longed to know the secrets of a Master Mason, and used the tools of their trade to kill Hiram.

Hiram went to his grave – dug by the miscreants – without revealing the secrets, and justice was done when the murderers were caught and executed according to the threats outlined in the oaths they had taken. But that was not the end of the matter.

Hiram Abiff's battered corpse was found and raised from the ground by a Master Mason. A proper burial within the confines of the temple was arranged, and a monument was erected to commemorate the way he abided by his Masonic principles even as he faced death.

This tale of Hiram Abiff's fate is acted out during the Master Mason ceremony as a ritual to represent just what a responsibility it is to rise up to the ultimate accolade bestowed upon a Brother. But it is just one of the hundreds of facets of Freemasonry that most people will never see or know anything about.

King Solomon's Temple was designed by Hiram Abiff whose death at the hands of fellow Masons plays an important part in the Master Mason ceremony.

FAMOUS FREEMASONS

Ever since the idea of Freemasonry started to become attractive to men who were not skilled in the craft of cutting and working stone, curious onlookers have wondered whether certain famous people were Masons. Through the centuries, many men of great repute and standing, from jazz trumpet legend Louis Armstrong to US author Mark Twain and British prime minister Winston Churchill, have been members of Masonic Lodges. Those Freemasons who have made their mark on the world are far too numerous to recount here – there have been thousands of them.

Within this chapter you will find some shining examples of the famous faces that have frequented Lodges around the world. There are movie stars, musicians, politicians and royalty, authors, astronauts and aviators.

From jazz trumpest legend Louis Armstrong to US author Mark Twain and British prime minister Winston Churchill – all have been members of Masonic Lodges

And remember, this list is by no means exhaustive – we are omitting most of the American presidents who have been Masons because there have been just so many of them.

Masons have risen to prominence in just about every walk of life. Many of the people cited in this section wielded great power or were fervently admired the world over. All have left their mark while subscribing to the principles of Freemasonry.

Some of these men did not make it very far upward in the Masonic hierarchy; others achieved great distinction in their Lodges. Some found Freemasonry was not for them; while others served throughout their lives.

From top left (clockwise): William 'Buffalo Bill' Cody, Franklin D Roosevelt, Clark Gable, Sir Winston Churchill, Harry Houdini, Prince Arthur, Sir Walter Scott, Charles Lindbergh.

Edwin 'Buzz' Aldrin

He may have lost out on being the first man to walk on the moon in 1969 – thanks to a change in schedule that put Neil Armstrong in that enviable position – but Buzz can still take pride in being the very first 'Mason on the Moon'. The astronaut is well known for his spiritual side and long term membership of the Freemasons – he is a member of Clear Lake Lodge No 1417, Seabrook, Texas, and was awarded the Knights Templar Cross Of Honor in 1969 for his space endeavours.

In his autobiography, *Return To Earth*, Buzz refers to Freemasonry only once – when he writes that he lost his grandfather's Masonic ring, which he wanted to take to the moon with him. Of course, there are conspiracy theories that Buzz did manage to take a Masonic banner with him and undertook a special deputation while up there – thus claiming the moon for the Texas Masons!

However, he was far from being the only Freemason astronaut; others have included John Glenn, who was the first American to complete an orbit of the Earth.

Above and left: Buzz Aldrin – the first Freemason to take a walk on the moon.

William 'Bud' Abbott

One half of the Abbott and Costello team that made some of the funniest movies ever made, Bud was a member of Daylight Lodge No 525, Michigan. His mother was a rider in the Ringling Brothers Circus – who were Masons.

Roy Acuff

The country singer was variously known as King of the Hillbillies, the Backwoods Sinatra and the Caruso of Mountain Music, and he sold more records than any other country star in the 1930s and 1940s.

Louis 'Satchmo' Armstrong

Hailed by some observers as the greatest trumpeter ever and one of the best-known figures of the 20th century, Satchmo is regarded as one of the founding fathers of jazz – and he was also a prominent Prince Hall Mason, which is recognized by some Freemason Grand Lodges but not by all.

Prince Arthur

Queen Victoria's third son – formally known as Arthur William Patrick Albert, Duke of Connaught and Strathearn – was revered for his dedication to Freemasonry. He was the longest-serving Grand Master of the United Grand Lodge of England, being re-elected 37 times until 1939, when he was almost 90.

John James Audubon

Audubon, who lived from 1785 to 1851, is best-known for painting and describing all the birds of America in his influential book *Birds of America*. Although no official records of his Freemasonic career can be found, he often referred to himself as a Mason and a 'Brother'.

Gene Autry

Autry found fame as The Singing Cowboy on the radio, in films and on TV, and no one who has heard his rendition of *Rudolph the Red-Nosed Reindeer* will ever forget it. Autry compiled the 'Cowboy Code', which included the Masonic-sounding: "He must never go back on his word, or a trust confided in him".

William 'Count' Basie

Along with Louis Armstrong, a jazz great who played piano and organ, composed, and led bands.

Irving Berlin

Another musical Mason, the great songwriter's works included *Alexander's Ragtime Band*.

Mel Blanc

The voice behind such unforgettable cartoon characters as Elmer Fudd, Daffy Duck and, of course, Bugs Bunny, his Masonic career was long and distinguished.

Jim Bowie

The frontiersman who fought to free Texas from Mexico and died at the Alamo was also famed for the knife named after him. Every year, a ceremony is held at the Alamo site by the Grand Master of Texas to commemorate Bowie and his fellow Masons, including Davy Crockett.

Daniel Boone (below)

This early American pioneer was thought to have been a Freemason.

Robert Burns

The poet regarded Freemasonry as the most important of Scottish institutions, and many of his works were based on the Craft. The Grand Lodge of Scotland boasts a painting by Brother Stewart Watson in which Burns is being inaugurated as Poet Laureate of Lodge Canongate Kilwinning in Edinburgh in 1787.

Eddie Cantor

This Freemason was a huge star of stage, screen, radio, and television from the early 1900s until the 1960s.

Andre Citroën

The cars are named after this French Freemason, who was a member of Lodge La Philosophie Positive.

Christopher 'Kit' Carson

The American explorer, guide, fur trapper, Indian agent, rancher, soldier and much more besides was a member of Montezuma Lodge No 109 of Santa Fe, New Mexico. The rifle he was carrying at the time of his death in 1868 was sent to the Lodge as a token of his esteem for his fellow Masons.

Samuel L Clemens

Better known as Mark Twain, Clemens was the writer who is best remembered for the characters of Tom Sawyer and Huckleberry Finn. In 1867, he presented Polar Star Lodge No 79, Missouri with a gavel made from Lebanese cedar. In his book, *The Innocents Abroad*, Brother Clemens refers to God by the Masonic appellation, the Great Architect of the Universe.

William 'Buffalo Bill' Cody

The founder of the *Wild West Show* that made its way around America and Europe was a member of Platte Valley Lodge No 15, Nebraska. In his former career as a frontiersman, Buffalo Bill showed true Masonic traits by treating Native Americans with respect and dignity, unlike many of his fellows. *Wild West Show* posters often portrayed the Indian as 'The American', and Cody was also a champion of women's rights.

Giacomo Casanova

If it needed to be proved that Freemasons can be great lovers, you need look no further than the example of Giacomo Casanova. The legendary Italian soldier, spy, diplomat, writer and amorous adventurer became a Mason in 1750 in Lyon, while traveling through France.

It is said that membership was invaluable to him as it gave him a large selection of contacts that benefited his future life considerably. Whether those contacts included some of the many hundreds of women he says he lured into bed cannot be stated with certainty.

This amorous adventurer made women swoon the world over.

Nat 'King' Cole

Crooner and pianist, who left his mark on us with such classics as *Mona Lisa* and *Unforgettable*, was a Freemason.

Davy Crockett

Another Mason! Crockett, like Jim Bowie, died at the Alamo after a distinguished career as a politician.

Cecil B DeMille

The legendary Hollywood film director and producer, known for the epic *The Ten Commandments*, was a Mason.

Jack Dempsey

Dempsey claimed the title of World Champion Heavyweight boxer in 1919. He was also a dedicated Freemason.

Sir Arthur Conan Doyle

The creator of fictional detective Sherlock Holmes was also a prominent Masonic figure until his death in 1930. He was a member of Phoenix Lodge 257 of Southsea, Hampshire, England, having been initiated on January 26, 1887. Conan Doyle made many references to the Craft in his books.

Edward VII

One of many British kings who have been Freemasons, Edward VII reigned from 1901 until his death in 1910. He was an active Freemason throughout his adult life, and brought the organization to prominence when he was made Grand Master of the United Grand Lodge of England in 1874, having been initiated by no lesser personage than the King of Sweden in 1868. When Edward ascended the throne, he assumed the title of Protector of the Craft, and his brother, Prince Arthur, Duke of Connaught, succeeded him as Grand Master.

Edward VIII

Another British king, best-known for his abdication after less than a year on the throne in 1936, Edward was Grand Master of the United Grand Lodge of England in that year. King George VI, who was well known for his dedication to the Craft, ascended to the throne when Edward VIII gave up his birthright for Mrs Wallis Simpson and assumed the title of Duke of Windsor.

Duke Ellington

The list of jazz musicians who were Freemasons continues. Ellington found fame as a bandleader, composer and pianist, and he was initiated into Social Lodge No 1, Washington DC – a Prince Hall Lodge – in 1932.

WC Fields

Famous for his starring roles in such films as *My Little Chickadee* and *Never Give A Sucker An Even Break*, the wisecracking Fields was also known for his fondness for the bottle and a love of pitch perfect one-liners.

Sir Alexander Fleming

This Nobel Prize winning Freemason revolutionized medicine with his discovery of penicillin in 1928.

Gerald Ford

The 38th President of the United States of America was a member of Columbia Lodge No 3.

Glenn Ford

The Canadian-born, American-naturalized actor appeared in 106 films, most of them westerns, and was voted number one male box office star in 1958. A member of Riviera Lodge No 780, Pacific Palisades, California, Brother Ford was awarded the French Légion d'Honneur medal for his actions during World War II.

Sir Winston Churchill

At 26 years old, the great war leader was initiated into the Freemasons in 1901. While he never actually took a position as an office holder, he was known to attend the Studholme Lodge on a regular basis up until his resignation in 1912 – the reason for leaving the Freemasons is believed to be because he wanted to focus solely on his political commitments.

According to Masonic lore, in 1918, Winston Churchill went on to sign a petition for the establishment of a new Lodge to be named the Ministry of Munitions Lodge – he was Minister of Munitions at the time. This petition, though, was rejected. The only record of another visit by Churchill to one of the Freemason Lodges was when he visited the Royal Naval Lodge as a guest in December of 1928.

Benjamin Franklin

One of the United States' greatest statesmen was also a
prominent Freemason. Printer, scientist and philosopher,
Franklin was initiated into St John's Lodge, Philadelphia
in either 1730 or 1731 and rose to be Deputy Grand
Master of the Grand Lodge of Pennsylvania in 1750.

Clark Gable

The heart-throb film actor, best known for his portrayal
of Rhett Butler in *Gone With The Wind*, joined the
Beverly Hills Lodge No 528, California in 1931. Gable did
not live up to the Masonic ideal of moderation in all
things, such was his fondness for tobacco, women and
hard liquor.

Sir William Gilbert

One half of the Gilbert and Sullivan comic opera duo (he
wrote the lyrics), Sir William Gilbert was a member of
Lodge St Machar No 54, Aberdeen, Scotland. His
Masonic love for his fellow man may have led to his
death in 1911: at the age of 74, he suffered a heart
attack following his rescue of a drowning woman.

Joseph-Ignace Guillotin

Although he advocated the use of La
Guillotine, Guillotin was not responsible
for its invention. A doctor, he was a
founding member of the Grand Orient
of France Lodge of the Nine Sisters.

Oliver Hardy

The much-loved fat one in the Laurel
and Hardy comedy partnership that
made, among other film classics, a
light-hearted poke at Freemasonry in
Sons Of The Desert.

Joseph Haydn

The 18th century Austrian classical composer is sometimes called the Father of the Symphony.

J Edgar Hoover

The Director of the American FBI who is best remembered for his anti-gangster initiatives during the Prohibition era.

Harry Houdini

The master escapologist, who died in 1926, was also a highly dedicated Freemason.

Rev Jesse Jackson

This much respected American civil rights leader and Baptist minister is a Prince Hall Freemason.

Charles Lindbergh

The aviator who made the first solo flight across the Atlantic Ocean – was a celebrated Freemason, belonging to the Keystone Lodge No 243, Missouri. Some have questioned how Charles's alleged Nazi sympathies could have lain easily with his Masonic life.

General Douglas MacArthur

The respected commander of the Allied forces in the South Pacific during World War II was eventually removed from his post by another Freemason, President Harry S Truman.

Tom Mix

The famous Hollywood cowboy boasted a long association with Freemasonry.

Wolfgang Amadeus Mozart

The genius Austrian composer of more than 600 works was an enthusiastic Freemason who used its symbolism in some of his compositions, including the opera *The Magic Flute* (see page 146). The son of a Mason, he was initiated in 1784 and was later a member of Lodge Zur Wahren Eintracht. His musical works included *Fellow Crafts Journey* which was penned to mark the occasion of his father receiving the second Masonic degree.

James Naismith

This Candian-born Freemason and educationalist was famous for inventing basketball. The sport's first equipment consisted of two baskets nailed to each end of his school's gym.

Arnold Palmer

The world-famous American golfer, like all good Freemasons, has become noted for his good works, including the founding of a hospital for women and children in Orlando, Florida.

Paul Revere

This man was one of the true heroes of the American Revolution, and was also a Grand Master of the Grand Lodge of Massachusetts. His dramatic ride to warn that "The British are coming!" was made world famous in a poem by the celebrated American poet, Henry Wadsworth Longfellow.

Sugar Ray Robinson

He wasn't the first famous Freemason-boxer (see Jack Dempsey et al), but Robinson found fame as a six-time heavyweight world champion. He was also a member of Joppa Lodge No 55.

Roy Rogers

This archetypal singing cowboy always wore a white hat to show he was the good guy. After his 1998 death, his gravestone depicts his Masonic emblem.

Franklin D Roosevelt

One of the Masons who rose to the presidency of the US – managing the feat four times. FDR was a member of Holland Lodge No 8, NYC.

Colonel Harland David Sanders

A Freemason who found worldwide celebrity. In the case of Colonel Harland David Sanders, it was as the founder of Kentucky Fried Chicken.

George VI

In a long line of British monarchs who have been active and keen Freemasons, George VI – who reigned from 1936 until his death in 1952 – stands out for his dedication.

He was initiated into the Naval Lodge No 2612 in 1919 and in 1922 was appointed Senior Grand Warden of the Grand Lodge of England. Two years later, he was made Provincial Grand Master for Middlesex. On his accession to the throne, he accepted the rank of Past Grand Master of the United Grand Lodge of England.

In 1936, George became Grand Master Mason of Scotland, and affiliated with the Lodge of Glamis, No 99. He oversaw and conducted the installation of three Grand Masters of the United Grand Lodge of England: the Duke of Kent in 1939, the Earl of Harewood in 1943 and the Duke of Devonshire in 1948.

George VI was quoted as saying he had always regarded Masonry as one of the strongest influences of his life. He was a Royal Arch Mason and was a First Principal: "The world today does require spiritual and moral regeneration. I have no doubt, after many years as a member of our Order, that Freemasonry can play a most important part in this vital need."

Sir Walter Scott

This Scottish novelist and poet famously wrote, "Oh, what a tangled web we weave, when first we practise to deceive." It is said to have infused into his novels a tradition of moral and intellectual well-being, manliness, truth, honor, freedom and courtesy – fine Masonic principles indeed.

Peter Sellers

The comic actor and Freemason who is best remembered for his contribution to British radio's *The Goon Show* and his genius in bringing to life the bumbling Inspector Clouseau in the *Pink Panther* films.

Jonathan Swift

The Dublin-born satirist, author of *Gulliver's Travels* and clergyman, was also a Mason.

Harry S Truman

It is said that Truman was the most active Freemason to hold the post of President of the United States. He was initiated into Belton Lodge No 450, Grandview, Missouri in 1909, becoming Grand Master of the state in 1940. He received a 50-year award from Freemasonry in 1959, and he was an Honorary Grand Master of the International Supreme Council of the Order of DeMolay.

George Washington

Have *all* great American political figures been Masons? It sometimes seems so. The first President of the United States was in power from 1789 to 1797. After his death in 1799, his widow sent locks of his hair to Freemasons throughout the country.

John Wayne

No list of film greats who were Masons would be complete without a reference to the archetypal man's man, the Duke himself. He stood for honour, truth, integrity and 'true grit'.

Florenz Ziegfeld

Broadway legend, showman and the creator of the Ziegfeld Follies, Ziegfeld lost much of his fortune in the stock market crash of 1929. He was saved by a revival of the musical *Show Boat*.

Rudyard Kipling

Rudyard Kipling, the author of *The Jungle Book* and much more besides, seems to have been active as a Freemason for only a short period of time, but his legacy to Masonry is large.

Living from 1865 to 1936, the Bombay-born Kipling was a poet, author and recipient of the Nobel Prize for Literature – and many of his works have Masonic themes. It is true to say that one of the binding principles of Freemasonry – that of brotherly love – appealed greatly to Kipling, who strove to express it throughout his body of work.

Kipling was the creator of some of the most spellbinding stories ever committed to paper.

MASONS ON THE EDGE

Is he or isn't he? The answer in many, many cases is "no, he isn't". Multitudes of men who have lived their lives in the public eye have been suspected, sometimes flatly accused, of being Freemasons and of wielding some insidious, bizarre mystical power over lesser mortals through their Masonic connections. They have ranged from politicians to movie moguls and from astronauts to comedians, and the misconceptions about them are manifold.

In many cases though, those 'accused' of being Freemasons with an agenda were not – and we will be examining these individuals in this chapter.

There is another category of people about whom there is a great deal of confusion: those who were at one time Freemasons but, for one reason or another, found themselves outside the Brotherhood at a later date.

Perhaps they did not live up to the high moral code expected of Brothers; or

Masons are, after all, human, and have failings; and some of these human failings will be laid bare in this chapter

maybe they abused their positions in the pursuit of power, glory, fame, sex or money. Masons are, after all, human, and some of those human failings will be laid bare in this chapter.

These people range from the errant US presidential candidate Wilbur Mills, who was better known for his drunken dalliance with Argentine stripper Fanne Foxe, to the automobile mogul Henry Ford, who exhibited behaviour that could not be described as brotherly love.

Then there are those men who were just plain bad and who also happened to be Freemasons as well. We will examine their cases too but, to begin with, let us clear up some of the common misconceptions that surround some of the past and present American presidents.

*From top left (clockwise) – Abraham Lincoln, Charlie Chaplin, Ulysses S Grant, Thomas Jefferson,
Lord Baden-Powell and Bob Hope.*

Not Freemasons: George HW Bush and George W Bush

The 41st and 43rd presidents of the United States are not, and never have been, Freemasons. There are those people who insist they are. Why? Could it be because Bush Sr swore on a George Washington Bible belonging to New York City's St John's Lodge when he took the oath of office in 1989?

This same Bible has been used for the swearing-in of many a US President, including Washington himself, Warren G Harding, Dwight D Eisenhower and Jimmy Carter.

Funnily enough, Bush Jr, the present White House incumbent, seemingly wanted to use the selfsame Bible but was prevented from doing so by unpleasant weather – it would have endangered the condition of the holy book. Nevertheless, in the eyes of many a deluded Freemasonry watcher, both the Bushes are Masons. Like father, like son.

While many US presidents in history were Freemasons, Bush Sr and Bush Jr are not.

"I did not have sexual relations with that woman." Such lapses in Clinton's 'moral rectitude' would not have endeared him to the Masons.

Not a Freemason: Bill Clinton

The popular but at times controversial William Jefferson Clinton, the 42nd president of the United States, is believed by some to be a Freemason.

But stories about President Clinton's membership of a Masonic lodge are wide of the mark. So, how did the confusion arise?

During his youth, Clinton was a member of an organization called the Order of DeMolay, and he achieved a fairly high rank within it. The Order has Masonic connections and young men from the Order of DeMolay sometimes go on to become Freemasons.

But this did not happen in Clinton's case. It is doubtful as well that the lack of moral rectitude shown by the President during his term in the White House would have endeared him to fellow Masons. If he had become a Freemason, would President Clinton have been shown the door?

Not a Freemason: Thomas Jefferson

We have to delve a bit further back in the American history books for this famous non-Mason. This founding father was the author of the United States Declaration of Independence and the nation's third president. He is not alone among early Americans in being thought, erroneously, to have been a Freemason.

Whatever else he did – and the brilliant Jefferson left his mark on the fields of agriculture and horticulture, architecture, archaeology, etymology, math, paleontology and other sciences, not to mention literature and music – he was not a Brother.

Some of his revolutionary colleagues were, however, and the name of Jefferson appears in certain contemporary Lodge records. The important thing though is that it is not *Thomas* Jefferson's name.

Perhaps it was wishful thinking on the part of some Freemasons, but Jefferson was not a member of the Brotherhood.

Not a Freemason: Abraham Lincoln

This is the story of an American President who was nearly a Freemason. Honest Abe, the 16th president of the United States, did seek to join the Tyrian Lodge in Springfield, Illinois in 1860 – soon after he was nominated for the presidency.

However, the application was short-lived, for Lincoln decided that it might be seen as a ploy to gain votes, and he withdrew from the Lodge. He never pursued his stated desire to re-apply.

Further rumours about his Masonic leanings surfaced when the Great Emancipator's funeral procession featured contributions from Masonic groups. The rumours spread to Europe, where they were accepted enthusiastically.

After Lincoln was assassinated in 1865, the Tyrian Lodge did pay tribute to his noble motives in post-poning his application to join.

Lincoln decided that joining the Freemasons might be seen as a cynical move to garner votes – so he did not sign up.

Not a Freemason: Ulysses S Grant

Maybe it was not for the lack of trying, but the Civil War hero and 18th President of the United States never became a Freemason.

Grant was following in his father's and his brothers' footsteps when he said, in 1871, that he was going to seek to join Miner's Lodge No 273.

A delighted Grand Master prepared to make Grant a Freemason 'at sight', but his preparations were in vain.

Ulysses died before the deed could be accomplished.

Death stopped President Grant from joining the Freemasons.

Not a Freemason: Lyndon Johnson

Was Johnson, the 36th President of the United States really a member of the Freemasons, as so many stories seem to suggest?

No, he was not – although, like Lincoln, he came very close to joining the Masons. In fact, LBJ took the initial steps towards joining the organization before he reached the age of 30.

Alas, he found his increasing workload as a member of the US Congress too onerous for him to consider pursuing his Masonic career. And he decided to leave it at that.

Not a Freemason: Ronald Reagan

Screen actor, Democrat then Republican, governor of California, 40th President of the United States, the Great Communicator, the oldest American ever to occupy the Oval Office – Ronald Reagan was many things, but he was never a Mason.

One February day in 1988, eight years into his presidency, Reagan met with a group of men from the Grand Lodge of Washington, DC, in the White House.

He accepted from them a certificate and was then made an Honorary Scottish Rite Freemason. His work was also recognized in the title of Honorary Member of the Imperial Shrine, conferred on him at a later date.

So was Reagan a Mason after all? No, the Scottish Rite is a concordant body and does not have the right to make anyone a Freemason. Neither do the Shriners. So you can call him a Shriner or an Honorary Scottish Rite Mason, but not a Freemason.

After all those presidents who turned out not to be Masons, and rapidly bypassing Vice President Dick Cheney (who is not a Mason either, despite the stories), let us turn our attention to men from other spheres.

Reagan was made an Honorary Scottish Rite Mason but he was never a proper member of the Brotherhood.

95

Not a Freemason: Sir Sean Connery

The charismatic Scottish actor who is best known for his portrayal of James Bond on the silver screen is also remembered for his part in the 1975 film *The Man Who Would Be King*, directed by John Huston.

This particular movie was based on the book of the same name by the British writer Rudyard Kipling, an enthusiastic Freemason, and we will explore its depiction of Masonic symbolism and philosophy later.

One of Sir Sean's later films, *The League Of Extraordinary Gentlemen*, is interesting for its use of Masonic symbols – especially the square and compass. The film itself offers a mythical blend of characters with superpowers. Perhaps the idea of Freemasons being somehow magical is still believed in some quarters.

Mason-watchers say that with so many references in his movies to the Brotherhood that Sir Sean must be a Freemason. There is no evidence to support this belief.

Sean Connery is mistakenly regarded as a Freemason because of his appearance in the film The Man Who Would Be King.

Not a Freemason: James Cameron

The director of one of the biggest-grossing films of all time, *Titanic*, is rumoured in some quarters to have received the 33rd Degree of the Scottish Rite during a bizarre ceremony at the Oscars. He did not. Cameron is not a Mason.

Not a Freemason: Walt Disney

So was the creator of Mickey Mouse a Mason? It would be a nice story if it were true but it is not. Like Bill Clinton after him, Walt was a member of the Order of DeMolay which, as we have seen, sometimes leads young men on to seek membership of the Craft.

In Walt Disney's case, however, it did not.

Not a Freemason: Neil Armstrong

Neil Alden Armstrong, the former combat and test pilot who commanded the Apollo 11 flight, became the first man to set foot on the moon, and the most famous astronaut of all time, on July 20, 1969. There seems to be plenty of evidence that his father was a Freemason, but, as for Neil himself, there is none.

Armstrong's Apollo 11 colleague Edwin 'Buzz' Aldrin was, as we have already seen, a Freemason (a member of Clear Lake Lodge No 1417, Seabrook, Texas), and so have been many other astronauts of note. They include Leroy Gordon Cooper Jr, Donn F Eisele, Luthor B Turner, John H Glenn Jr, 'Gus' Grissom and James Irwin.

Not a Freemason: Charlie Chaplin

There are more than a few sites on the internet where you can read that the ageless film comedian, director, and co-creator of United Artists was a Mason, but there is precious little evidence to support the claim.

Let us look at the founding of United Artists for some clues to the source of the rumours. Sir Charles' colleagues in the foundation were actress Mary Pickford, her husband Douglas Fairbanks Sr, and noted movie director DW Griffith.

But were not Fairbanks and Griffith Freemasons? Yes, they were. Does that mean then that the creator of the Little Tramp was a Mason too? No, it does not. Chaplin was never a Freemason.

There is one overwhelming reason why the English-born Chaplin could not have been a member of the Craft: to be a Freemason you have to believe in a Supreme Being, and Chaplin was an avowed, committed, lifelong atheist. In other words, not Masonic material.

His friends and colleagues may have been Freemasons, but Chaplin himself never was.

Not a Freemason: Sir Francis Bacon

He was a British writer, he was a statesman and philosopher; some folks even believe he was the real author of the plays of William Shakespeare.

There is widespread belief that Bacon was a Freemason, which he was not. Sir Francis died in 1626, well before Freemasonry in its present form existed.

Sir Francis Bacon died before the Freemason movement even existed – which means it would have been impossible for him to be a Mason.

Not a Freemason: Lord Baden-Powell

Let us give the British founder of the worldwide scout movement his proper title: Lieutenant-General Robert Stephenson Smyth Baden-Powell of Gilwell, 1st Baron Baden-Powell of Gilwell, OM, GCMG, GCVO, KCB.

Baden-Powell was not a Freemason. His brother was, and so was the man who followed him as head of the scouts, Lord Somers, but not Baden-Powell himself. Nevertheless, six Australian Masonic Lodges are named after him.

Baden-Powell (on the left) has many titles but Master Mason was not among them.

Not a Freemason: Bob Hope

Leslie Townes 'Bob' Hope has been described as America's greatest ever comedian. However, there is no concrete evidence to support the widespread claim that he was a Freemason.

The great comedian (and non-Mason) Hope with the 1940s film star Paulette Goddard.

Not a Freemason: Timothy McVeigh

One hundred and sixty eight people died, and hundreds more were injured, when McVeigh exploded a truck in front of the Alfred P Murrah Federal Building in Oklahoma City one April day in 1995.

McVeigh was an extremist, a terrorist, and a mass murderer. There are rumours on the internet that he was also a Freemason – even though no one has managed to come up with and verify even the name of the Lodge of which he was purportedly a member.

The internet is, as we well know, a fertile breeding ground for half-truths, non-truths and unsubstantiated speculation

It is not hard to discern how this groundless rumour started. The internet is, as we well know, a fertile breeding ground for half-truths, non-truths and unsubstantiated speculation.

It is perhaps depressing, given the seriousness and nature of the crimes committed by McVeigh, that such rumours are given credibility.

There is one vital piece of evidence that would automatically disqualify McVeigh from membership of the Craft. This mass murderer, who was influenced by Neo-Nazi, White Supremacist writings, has often been described as a Christian fundamentalist, and just as often as an atheist.

He would have found it hard, if not impossible, to be accepted in an organization that insists on a belief in a Supreme Being – and also tolerance and respect for any individual's religious beliefs.

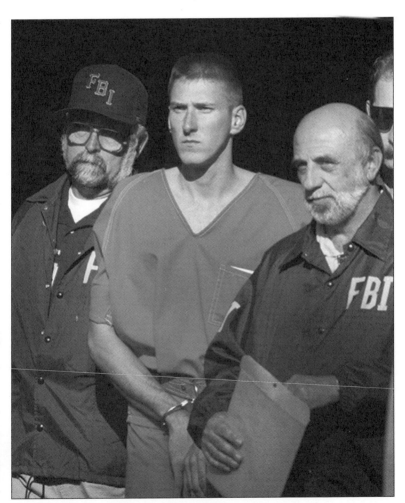

Timothy McVeigh – a murderer, an extremist, a terrorist but not a Freemason.

Not a Freemason: Aleister Crowley

Sometimes called "The Wickedest Man in the World", Aleister Crowley
was an English occultist, a mystic and a sexual revolutionary who died
in 1947. His reputation and behavior during his lifetime were not those
you would expect of a Freemason, so it should be of no great surprise
to learn that he was not one – even if some believe he was.

Crowley, aka The Great Beast, was a student of many philosophical and
religious systems from around the world, and went so far as to create
his own, which he dubbed Thelema. One of its principles was the
sovereignty of the individual will: "Do what thou wilt shall be the whole
of the law." Hardly a Masonic point of view.

There can be no doubt that some of the precepts of Freemasonry
influenced Crowley in his philosophizing, but so did elements of
Kabbalah, yoga and Buddhism. He did join a Grand Lodge in
France; and he seems to have been given the 33rd Scottish Rite
degree in Mexico.

The shame for those who link Crowley's supposed worship of Satan
with the practices of Freemasonry is that the kind of people who
bestowed these gifts upon him were not recognized by any true
Masonic authority. Crowley may have believed he was a Mason, but
the truth is that he was not.

Also, he was not impressed by the fact that Masons in London failed to
acknowledge him as one of their number, and wrote sulkily that he was
better than them anyway.

The Great Beast was not a Freemason.

Below are the cases of three men who were Freemasons, yet failed to live up to the moral codes expected of true Brothers.

Freemasons Behaving Badly: Benedict Arnold

Arnold (1741-1801), a major-general in the Continental Army during the American Revolutionary War, is best remembered for an act of treachery that has echoed down the ages: his plot to surrender the American fort at West Point, New York to the British in 1780. He subsequently fled to England, where he was rewarded handsomely for his loyalty to the Crown and given a commission in the British army.

General Benedict Arnold was under extreme pressure at the time of the American Revolution, and men under pressure can often crack

Arnold was a Mason for sure. So were many of his contemporaries in the revolutionary struggle, good patriots every one of them. But for his one misguided act, Arnold would today be remembered as a good patriot too.

Enemies of Freemasonry point to Arnold's act of treason as evidence that Masons are always up to no good. He did a bad thing, they reason, so all Masons must be bad.

Let us not forget that Brother Arnold was also under extreme pressure at the time, and men under pressure can often crack.

Heavily in debt, Benedict was facing charges of corruption from the authorities in Pennsylvania and, on the domestic front, his relations with his second wife were complicated by the fact that she was very sympathetic to the British cause.

Benedict Arnold is proof that every organization has its bad apples.

Freemasons Behaving Badly: Henry Ford

He founded the Ford Motor Company and the Henry Ford Company; he was a pioneer of assembly line manufacturing; he is said to have contributed to the creation of the American middle class.

Henry Ford was also a supporter of Hitler's Nazi Party and provided indirect financial support to the Nazi regime as it prepared Germany for war.

Henry Ford was a supporter of Hitler's Nazi Party and provided indirect financial aid to the Nazi regime as it prepared Germany for war

The following quotation is attributed to Ford: "The international financiers are behind all war. They are what is called the International Jew – German Jews, French Jews, English Jews, American Jews. I believe that in all these countries except our own the Jewish financier is supreme … Here, the Jew is a threat."

Such anti-Semitic comments are simply not acceptable in Freemasonry today. Ford though did join Palestine Lodge No 357, Detroit, Michigan in 1894. One suspects that if he lived today, he would never have made it through the Lodge doors.

Henry Ford may have brought transport to the masses but his indirect funding of the Nazi party brought himself and the Freemasons into disrepute.

Freemasons Behaving Badly: Wilbur Mills

A prominent Democrat member of the House of Representatives, Wilbur Mills ran for the presidency of the United States in the 1972 Democratic Primaries. He is best remembered, however, for his drunken antics with an Argentine stripper.

One night in October 1974, Mills was in the company of an 'entertainer' (Annabelle Battistella, better known to her audiences as Fanne Foxe, the Argentine Firecracker) when he was stopped by law enforcement officers in Washington, DC. His face was bloodied, apparently after a fight with Foxe, and he was under the influence of liquor.

Foxe leapt from Mills' car and ran into the nearby Tidal Basin. Surviving the ordeal, she went on to resume her career, sometimes performing under the name The Tidal Basin Bombshell.

As for Mills, after revelations of his alcoholism and relationship with Ms Foxe were made public, he was forced to resign from the Ways and Means Committee, although he later made a political comeback. He died in 1992. Wilbur Daigh Mills is one example of the Freemasons who have been judged less than perfect.

It is heartening to note that Mills, having faced his problems squarely, and taken steps to overcome them, and determined to better himself, was welcomed back into Freemasonry.

What of Foxe? She published a book called *The Stripper And The Congressman* and later returned to her native Argentina where, age 70, she is believed to be still alive.

Senator and Freemason Wilbur Mills; his dalliances with Fanne Foxe, the Argentine Firecracker, caused scandal in the mid-70s.

TALL TALES

For as long as Freemasonry has existed, there have been people who would really rather it did not. Opposition to the secrecy of the organization and a suspicion that there is more to the Masons than meets the eye have come from churches, from states and empires, and from individuals. Much of this anti-Masonic feeling has stemmed from the secret nature of the organization.

There is also often a suspicion that the brotherly love expressed in the philosophy of Freemasonry goes a lot deeper than just being good to one's fellow man for altruistic reasons.

Opposition to the secrecy of the organization and a suspicion that there is more to Masons than meets the eye has come from churches, from states and empires, and from individuals

These conspiracy theories have existed since the very beginnings of the organization and they will be with us until the last Freemason hangs up his apron and jewels.

It seems whenever there is a political assassination, an unexplained murder or a mysterious event that just does not seem to make sense, it is not long before the rumours spring up that the Masons are in some way connected. In the face of such opposition, this is the ideal time for a little reasoning to balance out the scaremongering.

This chapter examines some of the notorious incidents with which Freemasonry has been linked and attempts to make some sense of the conspiracy theories that lie at the heart of them.

There have been so many tall stories spun about the Freemasons that some regard the organization as if it were a legion of demons. Nothing could be further from the truth.

The Kennedy Assassination

It's a date engraved on the minds of many millions of people across the world: Friday, November 22 1963.

That was the day President John F Kennedy was shot and killed as he and his wife Jacqueline rode in a presidential motorcade through Dealey Plaza in Dallas, Texas. The details of the killing are shocking – half of Kennedy's head was blown away – and the shockwaves from the assassination were felt around the world.

Let us not forget that Kennedy, the 35th President of the United States, was at the height of his powers when he met his untimely death. He was young, popular, charismatic and powerful – America loved him. Let us not forget, either, that he was the fourth US President to fall victim to an assassination plot.

In the hours following the Dealey Plaza killing, former US Marine Lee Harvey Oswald, an employee of the Texas School Book Depository from where the shots were fired, was arrested and

JFK's probable killer Lee Harvey Oswald – a mere glove puppet for the evil hand of the Brotherhood, believe some conspiracy theorists.

charged with the murder. The proof of his guilt or innocence was not established, for Oswald never had his day in court: he was himself shot and killed while in police custody, by nightclub owner Jack Ruby.

So who killed JFK, and why? The Warren Commission, set up to find the answers, had little doubt. In its report of September 1964, the commission concluded that Oswald was the killer, and that he had acted alone. A further investigation by the House Select Committee on Assassinations, reporting in 1979, found that Oswald was indeed the assassin, but that he was probably acting in concert with other persons.

But the conspiracy theories, some of them involving Freemasons, have circulated freely ever since that fateful day in November 1963. One of the most prominent came from the pen of the late James Shelby Downward, who published an essay on the subject, *King-Kill 33: Masonic Symbolism in the Assassination of John F Kennedy*, which has been out of print since 1987. Downward's evidence for his claim is lengthy and highly complex. To sum up, he says Dealey Plaza, the site of the killing, was also the site of the first Masonic temple in Dallas – and the city sits just south of the 33rd degree of latitude. Every conspiracy theorist knows that the 33rd degree is the highest degree of Freemasonry.

Dallas lies just south of the 33rd degree of latitude, which is hugely significant to those who believe the Freemasons killed JFK.

Further, the plot of Shakespeare's play *Macbeth* – a king is killed following a plot hatched by three witches and his successor is then murdered himself – follows closely the twists of the Lee Harvey Oswald/Jack Ruby story. And the Shakespeare connection does not end there.

Mason Road in Texas connects to the Mason No El Bar and the Texas/New Mexico 'Land of Enchantment' border, on the 32nd degree line of latitude. When this line is traced west into the Land of Enchantment, it comes midway between Deming and Columbus – and north of Columbus

Did William Shakespeare foretell the assassination of John Fitzgerald Kennedy?

The three witches from the play Macbeth.

are the Three Sisters mountains, which are around 32 miles between Deming and Columbus and are just over a minute south of the 32nd degree.

If you trace the line further west, it passes the town of Shakespeare at a distance roughly equivalent to the distance which the 32nd degree line passes north of the three sisters mountains. Both Shakespeare and the three sisters relate to *Macbeth*, reasons Downward.

When the 32nd degree is traced into Arizona, it crosses an old trail, called Ruby Road, north of a ghost town – once called Ruby. The road passes north into the area of two mountain peaks called Kennedy and Johnson Mountains. Downward's theory comes to its conclusion with the observation that President Lyndon Johnson, a Freemason, appointed Earl Warren, also a Freemason, to study the circumstances surrounding the Kennedy assassination.

Downward further suggests that Gerald Ford, a 33rd degree Freemason, was able to suppress evidence of the conspiracy, and points out that FBI and CIA men J Edgar Hoover and Allen Dulles, Freemasons both, were key men in the supply of evidence to the Warren Commission.

Some believe that Downward's accusations are genuinely incriminating evidence of Freemason involvement in JFK's death. The more rational among us though might want a morereasoned analysis of such theories.

Let us start with the Shakespeare connection to the JFK assassination. Was William Shakespeare, perhaps the greatest writer the English language has ever had, a Freemason and was he foretelling the Kennedy tragedy in *Macbeth*? There are other claims that the great playwright was instrumental in the creation of Freemasonry, but there is simply no firm evidence to support them.

Now to address the theories about the 32nd degree, whether you interpret that as referring to the

Masonic degree, the geographical line of latitude or both. It has been pointed out, quite reasonably, by several sources that this particular line of latitude covers a massive area of the south-eastern United States and includes parts of New Mexico, Arizona

and Texas. Any conspiracy theorist worth his salt could spend endless hours inking lines of latitude with 'significant' place names and end up with a theory that could look reasonably convincing in print or on the internet.

So was the Kennedy assassination the result of a Masonic plot of huge proportions? Was Lee Harvey Oswald a pawn in the hands of a clique of Freemasons intent on ridding the world of this glamorous figure? Verdict: no, it was not and he was not.

The horrific aftermath of JFK's shooting as his wife Jackie Kennedy scrambles to get help for her fatally wounded husband.

Jack the Ripper

Jack the Ripper struck fear into the hearts of Londoners during the late 1880s.

During the latter half of 1888, the citizens of London, and especially its women, lived under the shadow of a series of appalling murders that has captured the imaginations of conspiracy theorists ever since. A serial killer who came to be known as Jack the Ripper took it upon himself to kill, in the most gruesome manner imaginable, a number of young women in the rather unsavoury neighborhood of Whitechapel, in the east of London. The fact that the Ripper's victims were prostitutes (or at least are believed to have been) did little to ease the fears of a population who earned their livings by more socially accepted means.

The killings started with that of Mary Ann Nichols on August 31 and continued with Annie Chapman (September 8), Elizabeth Stride (September 30), Catherine Eddowes (also September 30) and Mary Jane Kelly (November 9). The details of the murders were what horrified most: the victims were first strangled before having their throats cut; then their abdomens were mutilated, in a way that led many observers to believe the killer must have had surgical knowledge and skill. Annie Chapman's uterus was removed, while Catherine Eddowes' uterus and left kidney were taken. In the case of Mary Jane Kelly, the murderer left the scene with her heart.

The name 'Jack the Ripper' was first used towards the end of September when a letter was received by the Central News Agency. Signed "Jack the Ripper", it referred to a "leather apron", and continued: "I am down on whores and I shant quit ripping them till I do get buckled."

London's Metropolitan Police were baffled by the crimes, as they remain today but then, as now, there was no shortage of suspects for this most notorious series of killings. At the time, men under suspicion included Michael Ostrog, a Russian-born thief and conman; Dr Francis J Tumblety, an American 'quack' doctor who left Britain in some haste in November;

Kosminski, an impoverished Polish Jew who lived in the vicinity of the crimes; and Montague John Druitt, a lawyer and teacher who ended his own life in December 1988.

Of course, there has never been a shortage of theories as to the true identity of the Ripper, but one of the most controversial put forward pointed the finger at Queen Victoria's private doctor, Dr William Gull, who was a Freemason.

This story is expounded in great detail in Stephen Knight's 1976 book *Jack the Ripper: The Final Solution*. It seems the Queen ordered Gull to carry out the killings because the unfortunate victims had knowledge of a clandestine marriage between a prostitute, Annie Crook, and one of Victoria's grandsons, Prince Albert Edward.

Knight's theory also maintained that the seemingly ill-matched couple had a daughter and that Annie Crook was a Catholic – an issue that would have been met with horror by Queen Victoria as the head of the Church of England. The murders, according to author Stephen Knight, were carried out according to Masonic ritual. Throats were cut from ear to ear, left breasts were torn open, bodily organs were removed and burned – all these actions may be found in penalties associated with old Masonic oaths.

There is even more to this Masonic theory, centring on a graffito found chalked on a Whitechapel wall at the time of the killings which proclaimed: "The Juwes are the men That Will not be Blamed for nothing." Knight said the graffito was removed on the orders of Sir Charles Warren, a Freemason who happened to be head of the Metropolitan Police and who feared that anti-Jewish feeling would be aroused. But Knight goes further, claiming that the "Juwes" mentioned in the chalk message were none other than the killers of Hiram Abiff in the Temple of Solomon (see page 68).

Knight's assertions are based on the claims of one Joseph Sickert, whose father Walter, a Victorian painter, was in on the conspiracy and passed on the secret to his son. But does

Dr William Gull – royal physician to Queen Victoria by day, but by night some conspiracy theorists believe he was in fact Jack the Ripper.

Knight's story stand up to examination? Were the Ripper murders a gigantic Masonic plot to safeguard the reputation of Queen Victoria and her family? Let us take a look at some of the claims.

It is difficult to take seriously the suggestion that Dr Gull carried out these horrible killings when one realizes that in 1888 he was an elderly man of 72 who suffered from a heart condition and had recently had a stroke.

We can accept that the eminent physician had the surgical knowledge required to mutilate the bodies in the

So, were the Freemasons at the heart of the Jack the Ripper murders? The verdict: no, they were not

way described. Let's look at Knight's "Juwes" evidence. No part of Masonic ritual makes mention of "Juwes" and, anyway, English Masonic practice had removed mention of Hiram Abiff's killers many years before the Whitechapel murders took place.

Was Annie Crook a Catholic and therefore unable by law to ascend to the British throne? No, it turns out she was not. Was there a secret marriage between her and the prince? No records have ever been found to prove such a union took place.

But the most damning counterblast to Knight's theory came when Joseph Sickert announced that his story implicating Dr Gull in the crimes of the century was a product of his own imagination: it was a hoax.

So were the Jack the Ripper murders the result of an ill-advised marriage between an heir to the throne and a prostitute, and were the Freemasons involved? The verdict: no, they were not.

Queen Victoria – some have argued that she was the mastermind behind the Jack the Ripper murders.

Ku Klux Klan

One of the most commonly voiced accusations levelled at Freemasonry is the allegation that Albert Pike, one of the best-known American Masons of the 19th century, founded the Ku Klux Klan, that conglomeration of white supremacists noted for their racial hate and their tall hoods.

This is a serious charge. Freemasonry, as we have seen, declares brotherly love to be one of its major principles, and would not want to associate itself with an organization that has been, in its various forms throughout the decades, associated with acts of murder, violence and suppression against non-white, Catholic and Jewish people.

To get to the truth of the Pike/Klan controversy, we need to understand the principal players. First, who was Albert Pike?

Simply, he was one of the most important Scottish Rite Masons the Brotherhood has had. Born in 1809, Pike quickly made his mark: he passed a Harvard entrance exam at the age of 15, although lack of funds meant he could not complete his studies. He then embarked on a career that saw him become a teacher, publisher, lawyer, newspaper editor, diplomat and brigadier-general in the Confederate forces during the Civil War.

Along the way, Pike acquired an interest in Freemasonry and became an Entered Apprentice in Western Star Lodge No 2 in Little Rock, Arkansas in July 1850. His progress was rapid. He joined the Scottish Rite in 1853 and just six years later was elected Sovereign Grand Commander of the Scottish Rite, Southern Jurisdiction. He held that post until he died in 1891.

But Pike's longest-lasting contributions to the Scottish Rite were his revision of the ritual of that body and his masterwork, *Morals and Dogma of the Ancient and Accepted Scottish Rite of Freemasonry,* published in 1871. In short, Albert Pike was a busy man of considerable intellect and ability.

Some have accused Albert Pike, a leading Freemason of his time, of being a fully signed up member of the Ku Klux Klan.

Now, what of the Klan? It is important to realize that there have been three distinct versions of this grouping of like-minded racists.

The first, set up in the 1860s by Southern Confederate veterans, did not last long in its activities of intimidating freedmen, Northern carpetbaggers and others. The second, which flourished all over the United States in the 1920s, was inspired by DW Griffith's 1915 movie *The Birth Of A Nation*, which glorified the original Klansmen. Lynchings and burning crosses were its currency until it was dissolved in 1944.

The third, a group that is active today, declares: "We are promoters of white Christian civilization. We believe that the concepts of private property, free enterprise, representative government, parental rights, freedom of speech, right to trial by jury, right to address the government for a redress of grievances, etc are essential ingredients for a civilized and moral

The Ku Klux Klan ride through New York in what has become their standard costume.

The first incarnation of the Ku Klux Klan was set up by Southern Confederate veterans.

society. These are concepts born out of the genius of white men and women… When we give honor to these ideals we give honor to our ancestors and our white Christian culture."

It is clear, then, that the Klan does not believe in universal brotherly love; the love Pike swore to display. So why is he so often accused of involvement with the original KKK?

The claims stem from a booklet written by one of the original founders of the Klan, Captain John C Lester, in 1884. In it, Lester reminisced about the Klan but made no reference to Pike. In 1905, Dr Walter L Fleming reprinted the booklet, adding to Lester's reminiscences the unsubstantiated claim: "General Albert Pike, who stood high in the Masonic order, was the chief judicial officer of the Klan."

Susan L Davis contributed in 1924 with her publication of *Authentic History, Ku Klux Klan, 1865-1877*. She repeats the claim that Pike was a senior Klansman, without bothering to check out Fleming's highly dubious sources. These are sources that have never actually been corroborated.

Pike's name was never mentioned in 1872 Congressional hearings about the Klan – strange for a man who has been said to be highly placed in the original organization.

Critics of Pike's alleged hatred of African Americans like to point to a quote attributed to him in Delmar D Darrah's *History and Evolution of Freemasonry*, published in 1954: "I took my obligations from white men, not from negroes. When I have to accept negroes as brothers or leave Masonry, I shall leave it."

Take a look at the full text, though, and it is clear why it's helpful not to concentrate simply on parts of a quote: "The status of negro Masonry in this country was perhaps never better defined than it was by Albert Pike in 1875, when he said, 'Prince Hall Lodge was as regular a Lodge as any Lodge created by competent authority.

"'It had a perfect right to establish other Lodges and make itself a Mother Lodge. I am not inclined to meddle in the matter. I took my obligations from white men, not from negroes. When I have to accept negroes as brothers or leave masonry, I shall leave it. Better let the thing drift.'"

It seems that Pike, while he was perhaps displaying an attitude that would be thought racist today, was simply saying he had always been a member of a white man's Lodge, not a Prince Hall (predominantly African American) Lodge.

So was Albert Pike a prime mover in the creation of the original Ku Klux Klan? No primary evidence exists to say he was. But was he a racist? Judged by today's standards, yes.

This is how the Ku
Klux Klan initially
dressed back in the
times of Albert Pike.

Masons Targeted

It is not only conspiracy theorists who think that the Freemasons are the root of evil – over the decades, people with much more power did too. And with far more horrifying results. Adolf Hitler loathed the Freemasons as much as he did the Jews.

The persecution of Freemasons began on Hitler's rise to power in Germany in 1933, and it continued until his death in his Berlin bunker in 1945. Masons were threatened, sent to concentration camps and killed, along with all those others who incurred Hitler's displeasure.

The Masons, in Hitler's twisted view, supported the international Jewish conspiracy that was strengthening its grip on the world with each passing generation.

He wrote in *Mein Kampf*: "To strengthen his political position [the Jew] tries to tear down the racial and civil barriers which for a time continue to restrain him at every step. To this end he fights with all the tenacity innate in him for religious tolerance – and in Freemasonry, which has succumbed to him completely, he has an excellent instrument with which to fight for his aims and put them across. The governing circles and the higher strata of the political and economic bourgeoisie are brought into his nets by the strings of Freemasonry, and never need to suspect what is happening."

Strange, then, that a self-proclaimed Mason, Rudolf Glandeck von Sebottendorff, should claim in a book that Freemasonry had a great influence on Hitler when he was planning the dominance of the Aryan race. There is no evidence that Sebottendorff was in fact a Mason.

It seems to be true, however, that he did align himself with some pseudo-Masonic organizations in the Middle East.

It is equally strange that, as Hitler faced the prospect of capture or suicide in his bunker towards the end, he was kept company by a portrait of Frederick the Great of Prussia (1712-1786), who was a Freemason.

Adolf Hitler believed that the Freemasons were part of a Jewish conspiracy to take over the world and regarded them with utter contempt.

P2 - Propaganda Due

This particular Italian Masonic Lodge has found itself at the centre of a controversy with a long history.

A Lodge known as Propaganda Due ('due' is Italian for 'two') was founded in 1895 but was wound up on the orders of the Grand Master of the Grand Orient of Italy in 1976, after it became obvious that it was populated by men of uncertain moral character, some with Mafia connections.

The Worshipful Master of the Lodge, Lucio Gelli, was put out by the enforced closure and took it upon himself to set up a new organization called P2, even though the group was not recognized by any Masonic authority.

One day in 1982, the corpse of Roberto Calvi was found hanging from Blackfriars Bridge in London, his body weighted down by bricks in his pockets. The rumours about Calvi's murder, linking Freemasons to the murder, spread like wildfire, helped by the fact that the deceased was a member of P2.

Calvi was a banker from Milan who was involved in the embezzlement that brought about the collapse of the Banco Ambrosiano, which looked after a great deal of money belonging to the Vatican. Calvi, the bank's chairman (nicknamed 'God's banker') and Michele Sindora, a banker with Mafia connections, had been responsible for making around $50 million disappear from the bank's accounts. Calvi disappeared as the bank headed for disaster, before he was found hanging from Blackfriars Bridge.

There were further serious ramifications. Certain P2 members were also in high places in the Italian government, which collapsed under the weight of suspicion.

So who killed Calvi, and why? There didn't seem much doubt in the minds of anti-Masonic individuals, who accused Freemasonry of the killing. Masons were responsible for all the ills of the world, they reasoned, conveniently overlooking the fact that P2 was not a Masonic lodge.

Unfortunately for the conspiracy theorists, the truth seems to be emerging over 20 years after Calvi's death. The trial of five men accused of the murder opened in Rome in October 2005. Investigators believe Calvi had been laundering money on behalf of the Mafia. One of the accused, Pippo Calo, known as 'the Mafia's cashier', is already serving a life sentence for other crimes.

This man is alleged to have been the prime force behind the murder, fearing that Calvi could reveal secrets harmful to Italy's political and religious establishments. And how to explain those bricks found in Calvi's pockets? It seems they served a purpose no more sinister than to weigh down his lifeless body.

Was 'God's Banker' Roberto Calvi murdered by the Freemasons? Or killed because he was mixed up with the Mafia and money laundering?

So, was the death of Roberto Calvi, member of the non-Masonic P2 lodge, due to a Freemasons' plot? Verdict: no, it was not.

The One Dollar Bill

The US dollar bill features certain Masonic symbols. Does that mean that Masons control the United States government and its monetary institutions? The Great Seal on the back of the bill, familiar to all patriotic Americans, features an eagle with 32 feathers, clutching an olive branch in one foot and arrows in the other. There are 13 stars above the eagle's head and the Latin inscription below, E Pluribus Unum, means 'One out of many'.

The humble one dollar bill – it may not be worth much in everyday life but it's still a source of accusations and conspiracy theories.

It is easy to interpret this symbolism in Masonic terms. Some people say the eagle's 32 feathers refer to the 32 degrees of the Scottish Rite; an eagle is the symbol of St John the Evangelist, the supposed author of the *Book of Revelation* and a patron of Masonry; the olive branch can be associated with King Solomon, whose significance to Masons we have already seen; the arrows are symbolic of Solomon's father, David; the stars can be said to represent the tribes of Israel; 'One out of many' can be interpreted as descriptive of Freemasonry.

The other element of the Great Seal comprises a pyramid topped by an all-seeing eye, a symbol of God or 'the Great Architect of the Universe', in a triangle. Beneath the pyramid is the inscription *Novus Ordo Seclorum*.

The Masonic significance of the triangle, the pyramid (symbolic of the hierarchical nature of the Craft) and the all-seeing eye is plain, and the inscription has been read by some as 'A New World Order' – evidence, they say, of the worldwide Masonic conspiracy.

Finally, the front of the dollar bill features a portrait of George Washington who, as we saw in the Famous Freemasons chapter, was a prominent Mason and one of many American presidents who have been members of the organization.

Does the one dollar bill really contain evidence that the Freemasons are behind a far-reaching conspiracy for world domination?

The symbolism of the bill is to be understood in the context of the time when the Great Seal was first designed by a group of men led by Benjamin Franklin.

The eagle: the mighty bird of prey could be a symbol of St John the Evangelist, but it is also symbolic of the success of the War of Independence, of the break from British rule.

The bald eagle – a sign of pride, power and independence.

The bald eagle is a proud, powerful creature and symbolizes independence.

The olive branch: this is widely seen as a symbol of peace, and peace was exactly what was desired for the newly-fledged nation.

The arrows: symbolic of King David they may be, but they also represent the United States' readiness to defend its liberty and independence if the need should arise.

The 13 stars: they are the 13 original colonies over which the revolutionary struggle had taken place. There were 13 signatories to the Declaration of Independence.

E Pluribus Unum: this can be taken as a description of Freemasonry, but it is even more apt for a nation formed from many different peoples.

This is it – the back of a one dollar bill, the most controversial bank note in the world, according to some.

The pyramid: a symbol of hierarchy important to Freemasonry but also to the United States. The pyramid in the Great Seal is incomplete. The work of the founding fathers was also unfinished, for much remained to be done in the fledgling nation: the West had yet to be fully explored, for example. Take a close look at the 'western' side of the pyramid – it is dark, mysterious and unknown.

The triangle: certainly the three-sided shape has great significance for Freemasons, as we have seen. It also happens to be the natural shape of the top of a pyramid, and it often represents the Christian idea of the Holy Trinity: God the Father, God the Son and God the Holy Spirit.

The all-seeing eye. The Freemasons are watching you, it would suggest.

The all-seeing eye featured on the one dollar bill.

George Washington was a Freemason but not everyone involved with designing the Great Seal was.

They spy on every aspect of your life and are attempting to control your thoughts and deeds. But the all-seeing eye as a symbol of the deity was found in Christian symbolic imagery centuries before the very first speculative Masonic Lodges were formed. It was, and still is, a symbol of an omnipresent, omniscient God. Novus Ordo Seclorum: this does not mean 'A New World Order', but 'A New Order of the Ages'. Charles Thomson suggested the phrase and explained that the date '1776' under the pyramid was that of the Declaration of Independence, "and the words under it signify the beginning of the new American Era, which commences from that date".

George Washington: he was a Freemason, as were many prominent men at the time of Independence. Benjamin Franklin, one of the four men charged with designing the Great Seal, was a Mason also. But the three others were not.

Neither were the two other groups of men who followed up on the original committee's work before the Great Seal was approved.

Freemasons on Trial

Writer after writer have accused Freemasons in the world's police departments, and judges presiding over important trials, of supporting each other and trampling on the judicial process.

The British author Stephen Knight, in his 1985 book *The Brotherhood*, was one of those writers. He believed the interests of Freemasons meant justice was not done in many cases: meaning innocent people sometimes went to prison while the guilty were set free.

In Knight's view, secret Masonic signs are passed between judge and the accused in the dock, and judges and police officers conspire to ensure fellow Masons are found not guilty.

What Knight and his fellow detractors tend to overlook is that Freemasons are sworn to help guide their Brothers back to the path of righteousness if they stray. At all times, Freemasons must observe a high moral code, one which does not allow sending innocents to prison.

Cynics in the UK believe that judges are a branch of Freemasonry.

Cases like P2, Jack the Ripper and the killing of JFK are just some examples of Freemasonry being placed in the firing line. There are other cases:

The Bilderberg Group, which was set up in the 1950s to bring together people of international standing on an informal basis to discuss matters of import, yet has been accused of being a front for the New World Order under which a small group of men will rule the planet. Freemasons are behind this group say the critics. But where is the evidence?

In the street layout of Washington, DC. certain streets can be linked to form a pentagram, of mystic and Masonic significance. But Freemasons did not design that street layout.

There are numerous other myths, theories and alleged 'truths' linking Freemasonry with Satanism, and undue influence on the workings of governments, and judicial systems. They foment suspicion and hatred. They are not based on facts.

THE MASONIC MEDIA

The Da Vinci Code, Dan Brown's intriguing and multi-million selling tale of the supposed descendants of Jesus Christ, is only one in a long history of references to Freemasonry in the mass media.

The murder mystery novel makes several references to Freemasonry – some of whose members are said by Brown to be among the guardians of the secret of Jesus's family – but the history of Freemasonry, inspiring and informing works of art, literature, music, theatre and cinema and many other cultural forms, is a long and noble one.

Freemasonry has inspired and informed works of art, literature, music, theatre and cinema

This fascination has continued with the release of Ron Howard's movie adaptation of *The Da Vinci Code*.

Although a great deal of misinformation and misinterpretation has been spread by the authors and artists responsible for this massive body of work, many works of art and popular culture offer an unexpected and exciting glimpse into the world of Freemasonry.

They range from the Freemasonry-inspired musical works of Wolfgang Amadeus Mozart to the mysteries of Sir Arthur Conan Doyle's master detective, Sherlock Holmes. They include numerous references – some of them ill-informed – to Masonic practices, principles and symbols in the works of the Hollywood movie studios.

The Da Vinci Code *makes many references to the Freemasons. The book's popularity has been
further boosted by the film adaptation starring Tom Hanks and Audrey Tautou.*

Music

Wolfgang Amadeus Mozart, himself a Freemason, explored Masonic themes in several of his works, perhaps most notably the opera *Die Zauberflöte* (*The Magic Flute*).

Mozart was 28 and based in Vienna, Austria when he joined a Masonic Lodge in 1784, and he became a Master Mason at a time when the fraternity was under attack from forces within the Catholic Church and certain political figures.

The Magic Flute *does not*

mention Freemasonry openly

but its symbolism, its libretto

and its structure contain

familiar resonances

Nevertheless, Mozart set about composing his Freemason's Funeral Music and works for the opening and closing of a Lodge.

The Magic Flute, which opened in Vienna in September 1791 and is commonly held to be a Masonic work, was the composer's last opera, for he died – probably of rheumatic fever – just 10 weeks later. The opera does not refer unequivocally to Freemasonry, but its symbolism, libretto and even its musical structure contain familiar resonances.

Much is made of the number three, a number particularly important to Freemasons: there are three ladies, three boys, three temples, three solemn orchestral chords to introduce the whole performance.

Opera has been used to promote and explore the Brotherhood.

Audiences can pick up on symbols with which they would be familiar from Lodge meetings; the opera contains a number of references to Masonic rituals, and the opera is seen as a spirited defence of the Craft.

The anti-Masonic Empress Maria Theresa is portrayed in *The Magic Flute* as the nasty, scheming Queen of the Night, while the benevolent priest Sarastro is clearly meant to be the embodiment of an eminent scientist and leading Viennese Mason of the time, Ignas von Born.

Composer Jean Sibelius

composed works for each of

the degrees and presented

them to the Grand Lodge of

New York

But Mozart was far from being the only classical composer to have drawn heavily from the philosophies and rituals of Freemasonry.

The Finn Jean Sibelius (1865–1957), best known for his haunting, nationalistic tone poem Finlandia, composed works for each of the degrees and presented them to the Grand Lodge of New York as thanks for the part it played in establishing the Craft in the composer's beloved home country.

Freemason John Philip Sousa (1854-1932) made his name, and is best remembered today, as the composer of memorable military-style marches. He wrote *The Stars and Stripes Forever*. Other marches attributed to Sousa include *The Crusader*, which incorporates Masonic music; and *Nobles of the Mystic Shrine*, which is dedicated to the Ancient Arabic Order of the Nobles of the Mystic Shrine, aka The Shriners (see pages 42-44).

Jean Philip Sousa composed many Masonic inspired marches.

149

Modern Music on the Masons

References to Freemasonry are by no means restricted to classical music. Today's musicians, while they are not often identified with the organization, find plenty of opportunity to tell their audiences of their knowledge – or lack of it – of Masonic affairs.

The hip-hop group House of Pain, in their *Life Goes On* number, rap: "Did you know about the science of creation, About the Masons, about their nation, Of disarm, this arm, a leg or a head, To the thirty-third degree, you know that's me."

Those other hip-hoppers Run-DMC pay their respects to Freemasonry – perhaps unintentionally, in their video for *It's Tricky*. Here we find a young lady playing cards with eccentric magicians Penn and Teller and sporting a black 32nd degree Scottish Rite hat.

Country rock singer/songwriter Steve Earle might have little in common musically with House of Pain or Run-DMC, but he too name-checks the Freemasons. His masterful song *Copperhead Road* contains the lyric: "Now Daddy ran the whiskey in a big block Dodge, Bought it at an auction at the Mason's Lodge."

Of course whiskey is not served at Lodge meetings.

Country singer Steve Earle pens lyrics that contain references to the Masons.

Literature

When it comes to works of literature, Dan Brown is not alone in alluding to Freemasonry. One of the best-known authors who was also a Mason was Edinburgh-born Sir Arthur Conan Doyle, creator of Sherlock Holmes.

Doyle's works dedicated to the infamous fictional detective are full of references to the Craft. In *The Red-Headed League* (1891), for example, we find the following exchange:

"Beyond the obvious facts that he has at some time done manual labour, that he takes snuff, that he is a Freemason. that he has been in China, and that he has done a considerable

Doyle's Sherlock Holmes

novels are are full of

references to the Craft

amount of writing lately, I can deduce nothing else."

"Well, the snuff, then, and the Freemasonry?"

"I won't insult your intelligence by telling you how I read that, especially as, rather against the strict rules of your order, you use an arc-and-compass breastpin."

The Norwood Builder (1903) finds Holmes in familiar territory:

"You mentioned your name as if I should recognize it, but beyond the obvious facts that you are a bachelor, a solicitor, a Freemason, and an asthmatic, I know nothing whatever about you." Holmes is obviously familiar, then, with Masonic signs.

Elsewhere in his Sherlock Holmes novels, Doyle makes pretty frequent allusions to Masonic signs, grips, symbols and meetings.

"It's Freemasonry, dear Watson…"

Reference to Freemasonry in works of literature has not been confined to the English language. One of the great Russian authors, Leo Tolstoy (1828-1910), in his mammoth masterwork *War and Peace*, makes many references to the fraternity, and includes a description of an initiation ceremony. Tolstoy's research must have been extensive, for there is no evidence that he was a Mason himself.

Seekers after alleged Masonic intrigue should read *Two Crowns for America* by Katherine Kurtz, probably better known for her Deryni novels.

In her account of the background the American Revolutionary War, Kurtz keeps the reader wondering about the extent and influence of Masonic 'plots'.

She sees the war as the fourth attempt to remove the Hanoverians from the British throne and replace them with the Stuarts, and Stuart supporters use their Masonic lodges to guide the American colonists in this attempt.

Leo Tolstoy made many references to the Freemasons in War And Peace *including an actual initiation ceremony.*

That great British writer, Charles Dickens (1812-1870), gives exposure to Freemasonry in some of his best-known works, including *Barnaby Rudge* and *Our Mutual Friend*. In *Bleak House*, we find:

"Volumnia is charmed to hear that her delight is come. He is so original, such a stolid creature, such an immense being for knowing all sorts of things and never telling them! Volumnia is persuaded that he must be a Freemason. Is sure he is at the head of a Lodge, and wears short aprons, and is made a perfect idol of with candlesticks and trowels. These lively remarks the fair Dedlock delivers in her youthful manner, while making a purse."

Dickens' *Our Mutual Friend* has an equally engaging passage:

"Mr Boffin, as if he were about to have his portrait painted, or to be electrified, or to be made a Freemason, or to be placed at any other solitary disadvantage, ascended the rostrum prepared for him."

The American author Ernest Hemingway (1899-1961), Nobel Prizewinner, wrote *The Old Man and the Sea* and *A Farewell to Arms*. The last book contains this passage:

"'The Pope wants the Austrians to win the war,' the major said. 'He loves Franz Joseph. That's where the money comes from. I am an atheist.'

"'All thinking men are atheists,' the major said. 'I do not believe in the Free Masons however.'

"'I believe in the Free Masons,' the lieutenant said. 'It is a noble organization.'"

The characters in Bleak House *hold Freemasonry in the highest regard.*

If there is one writer who has raised making reference to Freemasonry almost to an art form in itself, it is British novelist and poet Rudyard Kipling (1865-1936). He made many allusions to and descriptions of Freemasonry, even though, as we have already noted, Kipling was a Mason for only a short time.

In the short story *The Man Who Would Be King*, a journalist on a train runs across two Freemasons down and out – Brother Peachey Carnehan and Brother Daniel Dravot. Carnehan

While Kipling was only a Mason

for a brief period of time, his

work contains numerous

references to Freemasonry and

its many secrets and lore

asks the author to take a message to Dravot. The story continues:

"'I ask you, as a stranger going to the West,' he said with emphasis. 'Where have you come from?' said I. 'From the East,' said he, 'and I am hoping that you will give him the message on the Square for the sake of my Mother as well as your own.'"

Later, Dravot exclaims:

"'Peachey, we don't want to fight no more. The Craft's the trick, so help me!' and he brings forth the Chief called Billy Fish."

In T*he Man Who Would Be King*, he writes:

"'Shake hands with him,' says Dravot, and I shook hands and nearly dropped, for Billy Fish gave me the grip. I said nothing, but tried him with the Fellowcraft grip. He answers all right, and I tried the Master's grip, but that was a slip.

'A Fellow-craft he is!' I says to Dan. 'Does he know the word?'

'He does,' says Dan, 'and all the priests know. It's a miracle! The chiefs and the priests can work a Fellow-craft Lodge in a way that's very like ours, and they've cut the marks on the rocks, but they don't know the Third Degree, and they've come to find out. It's God's truth.

'I've known these long years that the Afghans knew up to the Fellow-craft Degree, but this is a miracle. A god and a Grand Master of the Craft am I, and a Lodge in the Third Degree I will open, and we'll raise the head priests and the chiefs of the villages.'"

Kipling is here betraying an intimate knowledge of the Craft to a wide audience – and his use of that knowledge is by no means limited to *The Man Who Would Be King*.

In the story *Kim*, the hero is introduced with a Masonic reference. *The Wrong Thing* has the following revealing passage:

"'No, faith!' he said, 'only the Hall is as good and honest a piece of work as I've ever run a rule over. So, being born hereabouts, and being reckoned a master among masons, and accepted as a master mason, I made bold to pay my brotherly respects to the builder.'"

Kipling's use of Freemasonry's symbolism and philosophy is prominent throughout his works.

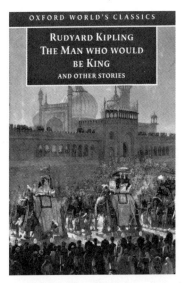

The works of Rudyard Kipling feature extensive use of Masonic references.

Movies

References to Freemasonry are not always very obvious in films. The viewer may not realize, for example, that in Oliver Stone's exposé of pro football, *Any Given Sunday* (tagline: Life Is A Contact Sport), the logo of the Dallas Knights team is an all-seeing eye and a Templar cross.

The use of Masonic and quasi-Masonic symbols in the movies is not a modern phenomenon, however, and goes back to the birth of the art.

Silent films like *Are You a Mason?* (1915) – adapted from a play by C Logenbrüder – are early examples. In this movie, starring John Barrymore, a couple of non-Masons try to convince others that they are, in fact, on the square. Then there is the 1916 movie *Bobby Bumps Starts a Lodge*, which features two buddies being initiated, and there are references to aprons and the third degree.

Freemasonry continued to feature after the advent of the talkies. No movie is better remembered for its portrayal of a quasi-Masonic organization than *Sons Of The Desert* (1933), starring the immortal Stan Laurel and Oliver Hardy.

The fat one and the thin one, sporting fezzes, are off to an eagerly-awaited convention of the Sons, which seems to take its inspiration from the Shriners. But before they go, they are exhorted to be faithful by their Exalted Leader, and the movie contains a typical contribution from Stan:

The ruler: *Do you all solemnly swear to be present at our 87th Annual Convention at Chicago?*
The group: *I do!*
Stan: *Me too!*

Needless to say, the boys' wives are not too keen, but after much chicanery Stan and Ollie go to the convention, which turns out to be a wild affair. The wives believe they are in Honolulu, and the truth is, of course, revealed at the end.

Even though Oliver Hardy was himself a Freemason, he was not above poking fun at the Brotherhood as exemplified in Sons Of The Desert *in 1933.*

Check and Double Check (1930), is notable for being the only movie made by the legendary radio funnymen Amos 'n' Andy. The duo belonged to the Mystic Knights of the Sea Lodge.

In the 1942 film *Across the Pacific*, starring screen legend Humphrey Bogart, judo exercises are performed by Chinese sailors, and it is explained: "Judo is more than a mere contest. Its devotees form a brotherhood, similar in many respects to our western Freemasonry."

There are more Freemasonry references in The Searchers, *a John Ford western starring prominent Mason John Wayne*

There are more Freemasonry references in *The Searchers* (1956), a John Ford western starring the prominent Mason John Wayne.

His character Ethan Edwards, on riding into a Comanche camp after a battle, finds a dead Comanche wearing a blue apron, approximating to the size of the Masonic garment, with a square and compasses sewn in white ribbon.

The 1960s were not fruitful for movie fans with an interest in Freemasonry, apart from a throw-away line in The Beatles movie *Help!* and one or two other allusions, but 1975 saw the release of John Huston's film of Kipling's novel *The Man Who Would Be King*, with its plethora of Masonic references.

Later in the decade, Sherlock Holmes made one of his many movie appearances in *Murder By Decree* (1979). Starring Christopher Plummer and James Mason and directed by Bob Clark, the film explores the London of Jack the Ripper and suggests that Freemasons might have been involved in some way.

Sean Connery in The Man Who Would Be King. *In terms of Masonic imagery in the movies, you can't get any more explicit than this.*

A fascinating glimpse of the Masonic square and compass can be seen in Mike Hodges' British movie *Flash Gordon* (1980) in which a henchman of bad guy Ming the Merciless sports the symbol on his uniform.

There is much Freemasonry in the 1982 movie *Secrets*, in which a Masonic ritual is enacted in the seemingly incongruous setting of a girls' boarding school. It transpires that the ritual comes from a book belonging to the dead father of one of the girls.

More and more Masonic

references were made in the

movies during the 1990s

and continued into the

new millennium

The square and compass symbol appears in the Mel Gibson vehicle *Mad Max Beyond Thunderdome* (1985), directed by George Miller and George Ogilvie (tagline: Two men enter. One man leaves.) As a fight scene is introduced, we see the symbol on the announcer's shirt.

More and more Masonic references were made in the movies during the 1990s and continued into the new millennium. The following is only a small selection of how film makers regarded Freemasonry in this decade.

Mel Gibson also features in *Conspiracy Theory* (Richard Donner, 1997), which contains the following dialogue: "'I mean George Bush knew what he was saying when he said New World Order, you remember those fatal words, New World Order? Well, he was a 33rd degree Mason you know and an ex-director of the CIA.'"

The weight to be given to this allegation can be inferred from the name of the film.

Mel Gibson refers to the Freemasons in the film Conspiracy Theory.

There are many references to Masonic detail in *Magnolia* (1999), directed by Paul Thomas Anderson and starring Jason Robards.

There are Masonic rings, talk of "meeting upon the level and … parting on the square" and Freemasonry books on display.

The Freemasons are once again

put in the frame for the Jack

the Ripper murders, in Albert

and Allen Hughes' From Hell.

In *Anatomie* (Stefan Ruzowitzky, 2000), a member of the "Anti-Hippocratic Society", which is described as a cross between the Freemasons and a college fraternity, embarks on a murder spree. The Grand Master is involved in the killings.

Freemasons are once again put in the frame for the Jack the Ripper murders in the Albert and Allen Hughes' directed *From Hell* (2001). Labelled anti-Masonic, the film implicates Queen Victoria's Masonic physician, Dr William Gull.

The villain in Stephen Norrington's *The League of Extraordinary Gentlemen* (2003), while attempting to start a world war, is seen wearing a Masonic ring.

More than the legend will survive.

JOHNNY
DEPP

HEATHER
GRAHAM

A HUGHES BROTHERS FILM

FROM
HELL

From Hell *starring Johnny Depp portrays Freemasonry as a force for evil.*

Digging for Masonic Treasure

Not all references to Freemasonry in the
movies are negative. *National Treasure*,
the 2004 film directed by Jon Turteltaub
and starring Nicholas Cage, presents a
positive image of its role.

Cage plays Benjamin Franklin Gates,
who is searching for a lost ancient
treasure said to have been protected by
the Knights Templar and, subsequently, by Freemasons. Many of the
American founding fathers were Freemasons, as the film is eager to
point out, and it is true that Brothers included Benjamin Franklin and
George Washington.

National Treasure is a good story, but it would be unwise to read too much
into its claim that America was built by the Masons.

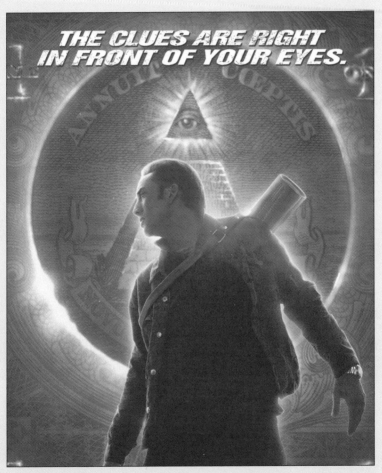

Were the Freemasons responsible for building America? Nicholas Cage's character thinks so in the blockbuster National Treasure.

Television

English language television has proved fertile ground for producers and directors on both sides of the Atlantic. One show that has won great acclaim and admiration worldwide is *The Simpsons*.

References to Freemasonry abound in the Simpsons' oeuvre, but the episode that has gained most fame is *Homer the Great*, in which Simpson père joins a fraternal organization called the Stonecutters.

References to Freemasonry

abound in the Simpsons'

oeuvre, but the episode that

has gained most fame is

Homer the Great

At one point, Grandpa Simpson says, sorting through some dues cards: "I'm an Elk, a Mason, a communist, I'm the president of the Gay and Lesbian Alliance... ah, here it is, the Stonecutters." The whole episode, a far-from-savage parody of Freemasonry, contains a neat song about control of the world.

The Simpsons returns quite frequently to the theme of fraternal organizations. In an episode called *Three Men And A Comic Book*, a convention is closed with the words, "Be sure to clear out by six for the Shriners". As Bart Simpson leaves the building, Shriners are seen arriving. In another episode, germs can be seen on Smithers' face singing, "Freemasons run the country".

Television offers much of interest to the Masonic reference spotter. A good example is provided by an episode of Bergerac, a 1980s BBC series, in which private investigator Jim Bergerac is called on to investigate an initiation ceremony that went fatally wrong.

168

Simpsons' creator Matt Groening is happy to lampoon the Masons – he knows they have a sense of humour after all.

Another British investigator, Morse, in the acclaimed series of the same name, came up against a Masonic mystery in 1990, when a murderer teases him by leaving Masonic symbols as clues, and Morse's task is made trickier by the Masonic status of his boss. Deepening the Masonic allusions in this episode, Morse, an opera fan, is performing in an amateur production of Mozart's 'Masonic opera' *The Magic Flute*.

Who could ever forget the

intriguingly-named Sgt Phil

Freemason Esterhaus in

Hill Street Blues?

A fairly constant theme in the equally long-running TV series *Prime Suspect*, again a British product, is the suggestion that there is a conspiracy clouding DCI Jane Tennison's quest for the truth. Secret societies and handshakes are mentioned as Tennison (Helen Mirren) tries to concentrate on the investigation.

Who could ever forget the words of the intriguingly-named Sgt Phil Freemason Esterhaus as his *Hill Street Blues* squad started to disperse to take up their duties in the 1980s: "Hey! Let's be careful out there!"

Interestingly, the character of Freemason displayed kindly, caring qualities to those men and women he was working for – as a good Mason should.

In *The Rockford Files*, the feelgood 1970s crime drama, Jim Rockford's (James Garner) father, Rocky, seems to make no secret of his attendance at Lodge meetings.

The Hill Street Blues *cast in the early 1980s. The character Freemason is far right in the bottom row.*

FUTURE IMPERFECT?

Interest in Freemasonry is at its height today, thanks to the literary efforts of the likes of Dan Brown and the *Da Vinci Code*, and movies like *National Treasure*. Much of that interest – both positive and negative – comes from mis-information and half-truths, and a great deal of it has been generated by injudicious trawling on the internet, where skillful editing is rare.

Alongside the opinions that others have of Freemasonry it is important to place the views that Freemasons have of themselves and their role in the modern world.

Many Masons would argue that the propagation of brotherly love, relief and truth are more relevant than ever in a world threatened by terrorists and others who have twisted the words of the 'Great Architect of the Universe'. And they would argue also that it is worth making time to do a little good in an imperfect world.

That excellent historian and statistician of Freemasonry, Paul M Bessel, in his speech to members of a Lodge in Washington DC not long after the start of the new millennium, said to the assembly: "Freemasonry could be, and could have been in the past, the only institution in the world that at all times in every way promotes tolerance and meeting on the level. We could be the leaders in seeking racial harmony, religious ecumenism, co-operation among men and women, civility between people who believe in different political philosophies, and friendliness among those who choose to live their lives differently from others."

"The only institution in the world that at all times in every way promotes tolerance and meeting on the level.

We could be the leaders in seeking racial harmony, religious ecumenism, co-operation among men and women..."

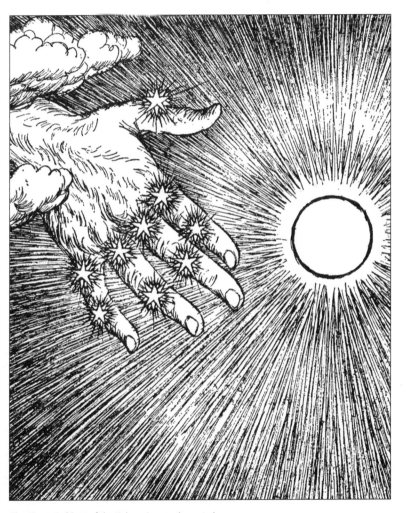

The 'Great Architect of the Universe' moves in mysterious ways.

If Masons are to be a potent force in the modern world, they must first address the problem of falling numbers.

Although interest in Freemasonry is at a high level, the number of members, both in America and worldwide, has been falling steadily since the 1960s.

Again we are indebted to Bessel, this time for his statistical work in tracking the numbers. In the US, Freemasons numbered more than four million in the late 1950s, but since that high point numbers dropped to around three million in the mid-1980s and continued falling, to a point where,

Membership figures have been

falling steadily since the 1960s

today, Bessel estimates there to be around 1.6 million American Masons.

In 1924, just over one in four of the population of the US was a Mason, he adds, but in the late 1990s, that proportion had fallen to about 0.75 per cent. The Masonic Service Association of North America says that, in 2003, Pennsylvania boasted the most Freemasons in the United States, with a total of 129,916, and Ohio was not far behind with 129,628. (At the other end of the scale, as might be expected, came Hawaii with 1,751 members and Alaska with 2,050.) Interestingly, Masons in Maine make up over two per cent of the state's total population, according to Paul Bessel, while Utah struggles to register on the scale.

The US leads the world when it comes to Masonic membership, but the global picture tells a similar story of falling numbers.

Around the turn of the millennium, Canada had about 120,000 Freemasons, England had about

360,000 and, slightly further north, Scotland had 150,000. But these countries' Lodges were similar to the US in that they faced challenges in attracting new members.
Many conspiracy theorists believe that the Freemasons society is nothing more than a religion determined to spread its word through the 'back door' and create control through its own self-serving 'church'.

In fact, to be a Freemason one must believe in a Supreme Being, and the Freemasons welcome people from all walks of religious life with open arms. Vehement anti-Freemason groups have accused the society of being Satanic, in part because of a series of hoax publications written by Leo Taxil in the late 1800s.

Taxil published eye-witness accounts that devil worship was a key part of Freemasonry rituals. Although he revealed later that these were made up with the sole aim of discrediting the Freemasons (who had rejected his request for membership), parts of the hoax are still used against the Freemasons to this day.

In the United States, there are an estimated 1.6 million Masons.

Critics of Freemasonry say more openness and a little less secrecy on the part of the Masons would be welcome, and there is no doubting that opening up a little could go a long way to dispelling some of the myths and misunderstandings, so attracting more people to the organization. The process has already begun.

Many of the Grand Lodges have an informative, welcoming website full of information on the history and future of Freemasonry; many hold open days, where a curious public can see past the seemingly forbidding doors and into the mysterious world of Freemasonry; many 'one-day classes', making it far easier to become a Mason, have been held throughout the US; many Lodges have ventured into the media with advertising campaigns on radio, TV and billboards.

It was not so long ago that the BBC was reporting thus in the UK: "Freemasons are holding a week-long series of events in an effort to throw off their image as a secret society. The doors of Lodges across England and Wales are being opened to the public, who will be welcome whether they roll up a trouser-leg or not.

"The United Grand Lodge of England hopes Freemasonry in the Community Week will help overcome the negative feelings many people have about the movement. Pro Grand Master of the United Grand Lodge of England, Lord Northampton, said: 'We are determined to dispel the myths and misconceptions that have surrounded Freemasonry for far too long.'"

This is just one example of Freemasonry throwing open its Lodge doors and exposing its works to the public. There have been many others throughout the world, and the internet has proved a valuable tool for communication. The US is leading the way in these efforts.

There are those who predict a long, slow death for Freemasonry, an ancient organization with outmoded belief systems that is no longer relevant in today's world. In fact, with interest in the Brotherhood at a higher level than ever before, with the growing realization in the Craft that more openness can be healthy, and with tools like TV and the internet at its disposal, it could be argued that Freemasonry has a highly relevant future. However, the Freemasons will probably keep a few secrets within the confines of their Lodges. They would not be Masons if they did not.

Freemasons across the world have set up websites inviting people to share in the Brotherhood.

The Light Side…

As we reach the end of the book, perhaps you feel as if the Freemasons take it all rather too seriously. It is all mysterious, stuffy rituals in darkened Lodges, with no time for a little light relief. And that is why no 21st century man would seriously consider joining. Think again.

Throughout the ages, Masons have been laughing at themselves, and they always will. Masons have a sense of humour just like everybody else. Want some evidence? What follows are gags told by Masons about fellow Masons:

Covering Your Brother's Back

A Mason has drunk just a little too much wine at a Lodge meeting and a Brother insists he stay the night at his house and travel home the next morning, rather than drive. When he gets home the following day, his furious wife wonders if he has been with another woman. Pretending to believe his story, she asks how many other brethren were at the meeting. "Sixty-five," the Mason replies.

At the next Lodge meeting, the secretary reads a letter from the wife asking if the brother at whose house her husband had stayed would please write and confirm that he stayed the night at his house because he was unfit to drive home. In the next day's mail, the wife finds 64 letters.

Freewheeling To Freemasons

On his way to the Lodge for his initiation, a candidate's car breaks down, so he decides to continue his journey by bicycle. At the top of a hill, his bicycle chain breaks, so he repairs it with a cord and freewheels down the hill to the Lodge. Later in the evening, replying to a toast in his honor, he says how proud he is to be a Freemason but cannot understand how the Worshipful Master knew he had come on his own freewheel and a cord.

Drunk And Disowned

A police officer who stops a man walking erratically down the street in the wee small hours asks where he thinks he is going. The fellow replies, "Offisher, I'm on my way to a lecture on Free... hic... Freemashonry, offisher." The cop asks, "But it's 3am, who's going to give you a lecture on Freemasonry at this time of the morning?" Our hero replies, "My wife, when I get home."

YOUR LODGE NEEDS YOU!

Perhaps this book has awakened an interest in Freemasonry and you are considering whether to become a Mason yourself. This is a serious decision requiring time and commitment and is not to be lightly undertaken. If you are absolutely sure of yourself, then go ahead.

The Freemasons will be delighted to have you in their ranks, and it is not as difficult to join a Lodge as some people would have you believe.

But first there are a number of questions you should ask yourself. Do I have the time to spare to attend Lodge meetings and to devote to good causes? Am I prepared to go through all that ritual, to commit myself to learning all the mysteries of Masonry – and to improving myself?

Many a Craft member will tell you that one of the main principles behind Freemasonry is to take a good man and make him into a better one

Many a Craft member will tell you that one of the main purposes of Freemasonry is to take a good man and make him into a better one.

Do you want to join a Lodge to have a good time and eat great food? While many Lodges do provide excellent festive boards, they are not the main attraction.

Another important question you should ask yourself: can I commit myself wholeheartedly to the three great principles of Freemasonry? Do I believe in 'brotherly love'. Can I show tolerance and respect for the opinions of others? Can I behave with kindness and understanding to my fellow men?

Will I be able to commit myself to the principle of 'relief', caring for those close to me as well as those not so close, and giving to charitable causes in terms of money, time and effort?

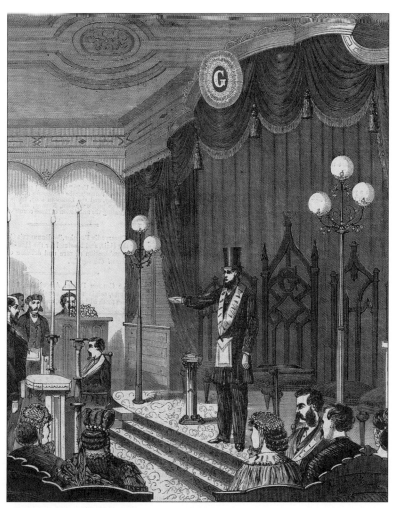

A Masonic Lodge of old, steeped in tradition and history.

To enter the Freemasons you must believe in a Supreme Being.

And can I strive for 'truth', displaying the high moral standards demanded of me by my brethren in the Craft?

Here is another important test you need to pass: can you keep a secret? As we have seen, Freemasonry is not a secret society, but it is a society with secrets, and they are meant to be kept.

If you have passed this phase of self-examination to your own satisfaction, it is time to think about the other qualifications required of candidates seeking entrance to the local Lodge.

Do you believe in a Supreme Being? If you are an atheist, you will not go far in Freemasonry. Remember, you do have to believe in a Supreme Being, but it could be under the name of God, Allah, Yahweh, Jah, Ishvara, Akal or any other nomen.

Even if you do not subscribe to a particular religion or do not have any name for your own private Supreme Being, that is no obstacle. We have to add one more qualification for being a Freemason: are you a man of good

repute? Or is your past littered with events that could come back to haunt you? Better to tell the Lodge now rather than later. Lastly, if you want to be a Mason you should be a man of a certain maturity. Some lodges accept candidates from age 18; others insist their members be at least 21. Have you passed the test? Then it is time to see how to join a Lodge.

To join the Masons you must be someone of good repute.

Putting Others Before Yourself

The object of becoming a Freemason is not to learn the secrets of the rituals. These are only a means to an end, designed to instruct the initiate in the principles of how to live a good life and in his responsibilites as a Mason.

There are some secrets in Freemasonry that you will be required to learn – and keep – if you want to go beyond those first steps to becoming a Mason. You will at an early point in your Masonic career be obliged to swear that you will "conceal and never reveal any of the secrets, arts, parts, or points of the hidden mysteries of Freemasonry… to any person or persons whomsoever… except it be to a… brother Mason or in a Lodge of Masons…" And that means you have to keep the secrets, arts, etc, from everybody, even your partner.

These secrets are mostly to do with the modes of recognition, the passwords, signs and grips that we examined earlier. But critics often accuse the organization of driving a wedge between husband and wife with its insistence on secrecy.

And some Masonic candidates find it hard to understand why they are told to take off their wedding rings before embarking on a degree. They may have good reason to ask, "Does this mean I'm going against my marriage vows?" No, it is part of an important ritual that teaches one of the first lessons you will learn.

You will at an early point in your Masonic career be obliged to swear that you will "conceal and never reveal any of the secrets, arts, parts, or points of the hidden mysteries of Freemasonry"

Your wedding band is not the only item you will have to take off. Other jewelry and luxurious items will have to go too, temporarily at least.

The Masonic Rite of Destitution teaches a highly important lesson, which concerns charity. The Rite of Destitution teaches that anybody can become destitute at any time and that, if you should discover somebody in this unfortunate position, you should help them to the best of your ability.

Becoming a Freemason does not mean the end of wedded bliss.

Finding the Freemasons

The Freemasons do not spend vast amounts of money on recruitment campaigns, despite what we have learned about the organization opening up in recent years as membership numbers have fallen, going so far as to advertise on TV, radio and billboards.

In fact, they do not engage in much recruiting at all, and in 999 cases out of 1,000, it is up to you to take the first steps toward membership. A candidate must seek membership of his own free will and accord.

Taking the first step is not difficult. A Freemason will make no secret of his affiliation if approached. Maybe you know someone who is already a Mason – a member of your family, a co-worker, a police officer, the guy who owns the neighbourhood convenience store. Or maybe you might notice someone you are talking to is wearing a Masonic ring.

Any of these people will take pleasure in explaining what is involved in membership of the Craft and providing you with the details of the nearest, or most appropriate, Lodge.

If you do not know a Mason there are other options for making contact.

Take a walk around the centre of your nearest town and, sooner or later, you will find a Lodge. They are not usually hidden away down an alley, and you will know when you are looking at a Lodge building when you see the square and compass symbol. Try knocking on the door, especially when there are signs of activity.

It may be that your Lodge is intending to have a public meeting in the near future. If so, you should attend and introduce yourself.

If you do not like the sound of this, maybe the internet is the place you should start. Almost every Grand Lodge has an excellent, informative website, and the same is probably true for your town's Lodge. You will find all the contact details you need on one of these sites. Just go to a well-known search engine such as Google or Yahoo, type in the name of your town and any of these words:

Freemason, Masonic, Lodge. Once you have found your Lodge, and future fellow Masons, you can begin the joining process.

The Freemasons are not some clandestine organization that will need hunting out by a professional.

Joining the Freemasons

The Brotherhood does not let just anyone join because they want to. There is a selection process you need to go through first.

To begin with, you need to petition to join the Lodge. On the petition form, there will be questions that you will need to answer truthfully.

Answer the committee's questions in the honest spirit in which they are asked, and you can also use the occasion to pose any questions of your own

Also, you will need the recommendation of two existing Masons. Your petition will be considered at a meeting of the Lodge, which will then appoint a committee to meet you.

Again, answer the committee's questions in the honest spirit in which they are asked, and you can also use the occasion to pose any questions of your own.

It will not be long before the committee reports back to the Lodge with its findings, and then it is time for your petition to be tested in the form of a secret ballot.

If the vote goes the way you are hoping, a date will then be set for your actual admission to the Lodge, and it will be time to prepare for the initiation ceremony.

One day you may finally become a Master Mason.

A secret ballot takes place to see if the Freemasons' committee wishes to admit you as an apprentice.

Now you are a Freemason

There are many reasons for becoming a Freemason. You are now a member of a global fraternal organization that offers good companionship and enjoyable times. Your new brethren will do their best to ensure you enjoy your Masonic career.

If you are the kind of man who relishes a challenge, you will find plenty in Freemasonry to satisfy you. You will be learning not only about the secrets, traditions and principles of the Craft but also invaluable lessons about yourself. You will learn the true worth of humility; your very first participation in a Masonic ritual, hoodwinked and with flesh exposed, will ensure that.

You will be encouraged to conduct yourself in a way that will set you on the path to self-fulfillment via your chosen path. And, when you take part in Lodge meetings and the dramatic portrayal of moral lessons, you will be learning how to improve yourself. Good as they are, those are just some of the reasons to think about becoming a Freemason.

You will learn that you are expected to help your brethren in times of need, and that your brethren will likewise help you.

You might benefit from the services of a Masonic retirement home when the time comes. You will be able to channel your love for your fellow man and woman into charitable works, for the benefit of your community and others less fortunate than yourself.

It does not matter whether you are rich or poor, for in the Brotherhood, all Masons are equal.

You will learn that you are expected to help your brethren in times of need, and that your brethren will likewise help you

PICTURE CREDITS